Practice Workbook

ISBN: 0-13-435822-8

Printed in the United States of America.

10 11 12 13   04 03 02

PRENTICE HALL

Upper Saddle River, New Jersey • Needham Heights, Massachusetts

Practice Workbook

Contents

Answers for practice worksheets appear with each lesson in the *Teacher's Edition* as well as in the back of each Chapter Support File.

◾▬ *Practice*

For use after 1-1 (pp. 4–7)

Integers

Give an integer to represent each situation.

1. a loss of $70 _________

2. a temperature of 42° above 0 _________

3. an elevator goes down 16 floors _________

4. an increase of 213 _________

Write each integer.

5. the opposite of 17 _________

6. $|-9|$ _________

7. $|21|$ _________

8. the opposite of -8 _________

9. $|0|$ _________

10. $|-1|$ _________

11. the absolute value of the opposite of negative 5 _________

12. the absolute value of the opposite of 11 _________

Write the integer for each point on the number line.

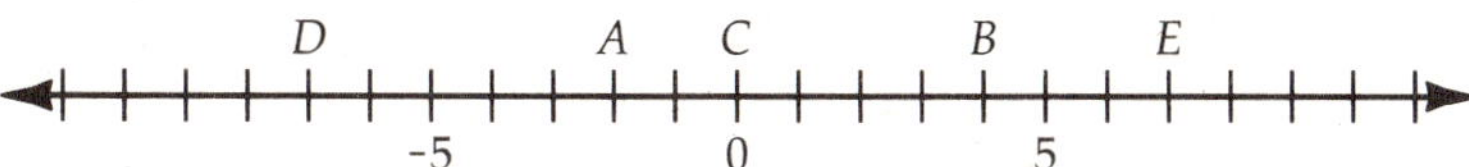

13. A _________   14. B _________   15. C _________   16. D _________   17. E _________

Graph each integer on the number line.

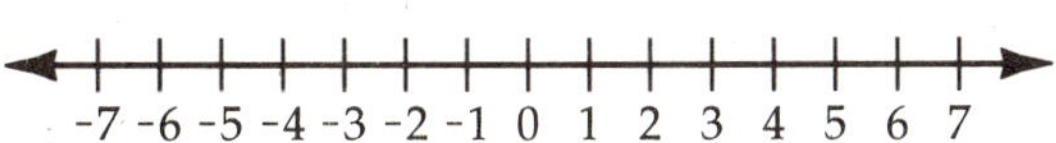

18. -6 19. 2   20. $|-4|$ 21. $|7|$ 22. $-|-3|$

Compare. Use >, <, or =.

23. $-3 \bigcirc 4$ 24. $5 \bigcirc 1$ 25. $-2 \bigcirc -6$ 26. $7 \bigcirc |8|$

27. $|-2| \bigcirc |2|$ 28. $|-1| \bigcirc -6$ 29. $|4| \bigcirc |-5|$ 30. $0 \bigcirc |-7|$

True or false?

31. All integers are negative. _________

32. The absolute value of every integer is its opposite. _________

33. Two integers that are opposites have the same absolute value. _________

34. The absolute value of an integer is always positive. _________

35. The opposite of an integer is always negative. _________

36. The absolute value of a postive integer is the integer. _________

37. The absolute value of an integer is always greater than the integer. _________

38. A positive and negative integer will always add to zero. _________

Practice

Adding Integers

Write a numerical expression for each situation. Find the sum.

1. climb up 26 steps, then climb down 9 steps ________________________________

2. earn $100, spend $62, earn $35, spend $72 ________________________________

Draw a model to represent each number sentence.

3. $-7 + 6 = -1$

4. $3 + (-6) + 4 = 1$

Write an equation to represent each sum on the number line.

5. 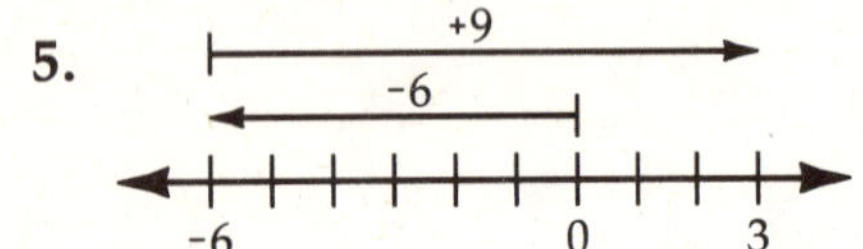

6. 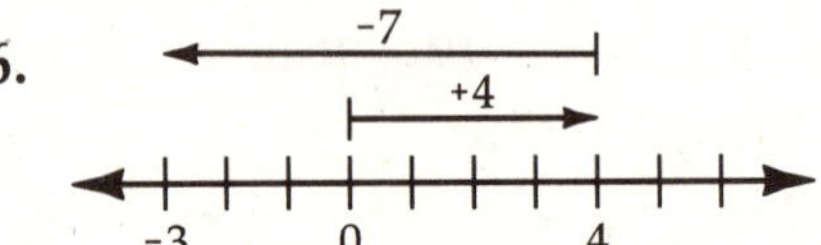

____

____

7. 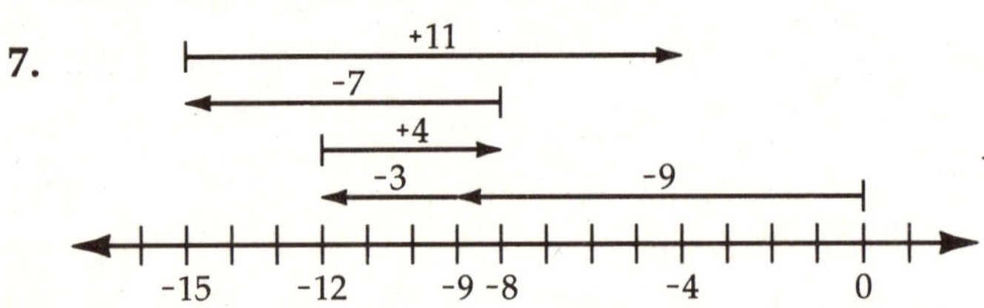

____

MENTAL MATH **Find each sum mentally.**

8. $-8 + 8 + -11$ ________

9. $-15 + 7 + 15$ ________

10. $12 + (-7) + 3 + (-8)$ ________

11. $-5 + (-16) + 5 + 8 + 16$ ________

CALCULATOR **Find each sum.**

12. $192 + (-129)$ ________

13. $-417 + (-296)$ ________

14. $-87 + 175$ ________

Find each sum. Choose a method to use.

15. $-8 + (-3)$ ________

16. $6 + (-6)$ ________

17. $-12 + (-17)$ ________

18. $9 + (-11)$ ________

19. $-4 + (-6)$ ________

20. $18 + (-17)$ ________

Compare. Write >, <, or =.

21. $-7 + 5 \bigcirc 3 + (-6)$

22. $4 + (-9) \bigcirc 6 + (-7) + (-4)$

23. An elevator went up 15 floors, down 9 floors, up 11 floors, and down 19 floors. Find the net change. ________________________

Practice

Subtracting Integers

Write a number sentence for each number line.

1. 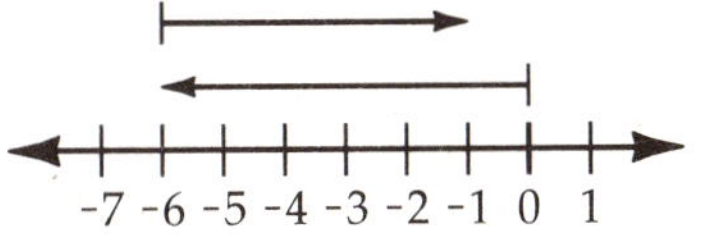

   ____

2. 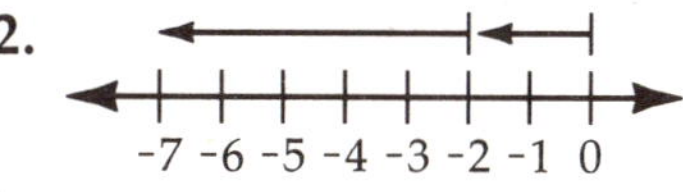

   ____

Draw an algebra model to represent each number sentence.

3. $4 - (-3) = 7$

4. $-6 - (-5) = -1$

Write a numerical expression for each phrase.

5. A balloon goes up 2,300 ft, then goes down 600 ft. _______________________________

6. You lose $50, then spend $35. _______________________________

MENTAL MATH Find each difference.

7. $6 - 9$ _________

8. $14 - 8$ _________

9. $-15 - 3$ _________

10. $-25 - 25$ _________

11. $-16 - (-16)$ _________

12. $32 - (-17) - 32$ _________

CALCULATOR Find each difference.

13. $51 - 89$ _________

14. $-222 - (-117)$ _________

15. $843 - 677$ _________

16. $-98 - 183$ _________

17. $366 - (-429)$ _________

18. $-83 - (-48) - 65$ _________

Find each difference. Use any method you wish.

19. $8 - 12$ _________

20. $13 - 6$ _________

21. $9 - (-12)$ _________

22. $57 - 39$ _________

23. $-173 - 162$ _________

24. $71 - (123)$ _________

25. $|-71| - |83|$ _________

26. $48 - |-116|$ _________

27. $-|275| - |-175|$ _________

ESTIMATION Round each number to a convenient place. Estimate the answer.

28. $-57 + (-98)$ _________

29. $448 - 52$ _________

30. $-191 + (-511)$ _________

31. $-361 - (-58)$ _________

32. $888 + 1,177$ _________

33. $-484 - 1,695$ _________

Solve.

34. The Glasers had $317 in their checking account. They wrote checks for $74, $132, and $148. By how much was their account overdrawn? _________

Practice

Look for a Pattern

Use the given numbers to find a pattern. Then write the next three numbers in the pattern.

1. 3, 6, 9, 12, 15, _______ , _______ , _______

2. 1, 2, 4, 8, 16, _______ , _______ , _______

3. 6, 7, 14, 15, 30, 31, _______ , _______ , _______

4. 27, 33, 39, 45, 51, _______ , _______ , _______

5. 1, 4, 16, 64, _______ , _______ , _______

6. 34, 27, 20, 13, 6, _______ , _______ , _______

7. Each row in a window display of floppy disk cartons contains two more boxes than the row above.

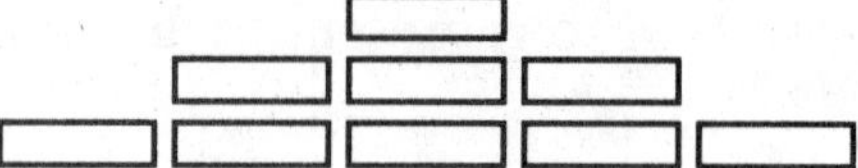

a. Complete the table.

Row number	1	2	3	4	5	6
Total boxes in the display						

b. Describe the pattern in the numbers you wrote. _______________________________________

____

____

c. Find the number of rows in a display containing the given number of boxes.

81 _________   144 _________   400 _________

d. Describe how you can use the number of boxes in the

display to calculate the number of rows. _______________________________________

____

8. A computer multiplied 9 by itself 100 times. You can use patterns to find the ones' digit of the product.

$$9 \times \underbrace{9 \times 9 \times 9 \times 9 \times \cdots \times 9}_{100 \text{ times}}$$

a. Find the ones' digit when 9 is multiplied by itself:

1 time _________   2 times _________   3 times _________   4 times _________

b. Describe the pattern. _______________________________________

____

____

c. What is the ones' digit of the computer product? _________

9. Use the method of Exercise 8 to find the ones' digit of the product when 4 is multiplied by itself 100 times. _________

Practice

Multiplying Integers

Use repeated addition to find each product.

1. −3(5) _________ **2.** 4(−5) _________ **3.** 6(−2) _________ **4.** −15 • 3 _________

Use patterns to find each product.

5. −5(−2) _________ **6.** −7(−4) _________ **7.** −3(−8) _________ **8.** −9(−6) _________

CALCULATOR **Find each product.**

9. −36(29) _________ **10.** −117(−89) _________ **11.** −7(−56)(−13) _________

Find each answer. Choose a method to use.

12. −9(−2) _________ **13.** 0(−7) _________ **14.** 6(−8) _________

15. −12(−10) _________ **16.** −29(−1) _________ **17.** −2(−2)(7) _________

18. −17 • 3 _________ **19.** 8 • 7(−6) _________ **20.** −14|−3| _________

21. −7 • 50 _________ **22.** |−18| • |18| _________ **23.** 23 • 16 _________

Write a numerical expression for each phrase. Then find the product.

24. the opposite of nine times negative seven _____________________________

25. the product of the absolute value of negative twelve and the opposite of

five _____________________________

26. six times the product of negative eight and the opposite of three

____

27. the absolute value of negative nine times the sum of five and negative

two _____________________________

28. the opposite of the product of thirty and negative four

____

Compare. Use >, <, or = to make a true statement.

29. −3(3) ◯ 4(−2) **30.** |−5| • |−7| ◯ 6(−6) **31.** −1(2) ◯ −3(0)

32. −3(3) ◯ −13 **33.** 49 • 2 ◯ (−49)(−2) **34.** 6(2 • 3) ◯ 2 • 3

Solve.

35. The Red Sox fell 3 games farther back in the league standings each week
for 7 consecutive weeks. Use an integer to represent the team's total

drop in the standings. _________

▬▬ *Practice*

Dividing Integers

Find each quotient. Write a related multiplication sentence.

1. $-36 \div (-4)$ _________________

2. $30 \div (-5)$ _________________

MENTAL MATH Find each quotient.

3. $16 \div (-2)$ _________

4. $-35 \div (-7)$ _________

5. $-80 \div 10$ _________

CALCULATOR Find each quotient.

6. $-299 \div 13$ _________

7. $255 \div 15$ _________

8. $-779 \div (-19)$ _________

Find each answer. Choose a method to use.

9. $54 \div (-9)$ _________

10. $-37 \div (-1)$ _________

11. $91 \div 7$ _________

12. $77 \div (-77)$ _________

13. $-416 \div 52$ _________

14. $0 \div (-95)$ _________

15. $-2,500 \div 25$ _________

16. $-363 \div (-33)$ _________

17. $21 \div (-7)$ _________

18. $-200 \div 5$ _________

19. $5,984 \div (-68)$ _________

20. $72 \div 9$ _________

Write a numerical expression for each word phrase. Then evaluate the expression.

21. the opposite of forty-nine divided by the opposite of seven _________________

22. negative eighty-eight divided by the absolute value of negative forty-four _________________

Find the mean.

23. stock price changes: $+\$3$, $+\$7$, $-\$5$, $+\$4$, $-\$12$, $\$9$ _________

24. scores: 377, 161, -418, -529, 485, -771, 654, -463 _________

25. weight changes: $+2$, -10, -3, $+14$, -1, $+5$, -9, -6 _________

Write $>$, $<$, or $=$ to make a true statement.

26. $-18 \div 9 \bigcirc 36 \div (-12)$

27. $-|35 \div (-7)| \bigcirc -60 \div (-12)$

28. $108 \div 9 \bigcirc 24 \div 2$

29. $|33 \div (-3)| \bigcirc 50 \div 10$

Solve.

30. An integer multiplied by 18 equals -90. What is the integer? _________

31. At 1 A.M. the temperature was $-17°$F. At 5 A.M. it had dropped to $-53°$F. Find the average change in temperature per hour. _________

Practice

Expressions and Variables

Write a variable expression for each model.

1. 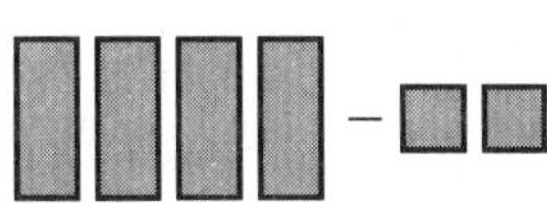

2. 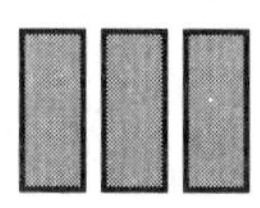

3. 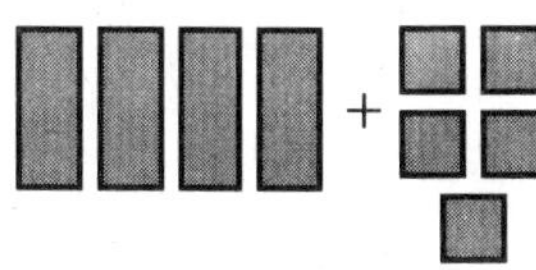

_______________   _______________   _______________

Draw a model to represent each variable expression.

4. $3y + 4$

5. $-3 - n$

Write a numerical expression for each word phrase.

6. five less than the opposite of nine _________

7. the product of eight and negative six _________

Write a variable expression for each word phrase.

8. the sum of x and y _____________

9. p divided by k _____________

10. h less than negative two _____________

11. x times g _____________

12. eleven more than z _____________

13. three increased by twice h _____________

Write two different word phrases for each variable expression.

14. $g + 7$ ____

15. $n \div 3$ ____

Write a variable expression for each situation.

16. the number of minutes in h hours _________

17. the value, in cents, of d dimes _________

18. the number of inches in f feet _________

19. the number of hours in d days _________

A book contains p pages. Write an expression for the number of pages in a book:

20. with 35 fewer pages _________

21. longer by 82 pages _________

22. with three times as many pages

____

23. with 26 more than double the

number of pages _________

24. with 32 less than double the

number of pages _________

25. with one third as many pages

____

Practice

For use after 1-9 (pp. 40–43)

Order of Operations

Which operation would you perform first? Explain.

1. $25 - 16 \div 4 \times 2 + 6$ ____

____

2. $16 \div (10 - 2) \cdot 5$ ____

Evaluate.

3. $24 - 16 + 5$ _______ **4.** $20 \div 2 \cdot 5$ _______ **5.** $9 + 6 \div 3$ _______

6. $4 + (-3) \cdot 5$ _______ **7.** $-19 + 20 \div (-2)$ _______ **8.** $-3 - |4 - 10|$ _______

MENTAL MATH **Evaluate.**

9. $14 - 6 - 3$ _______ **10.** $14 - (6 - 3)$ _______ **11.** $-6 \cdot 4 \div (-2)$ _______

12. $-2 \cdot 5 + 3 \cdot (-6)$ _______ **13.** $5 - 42 \div (-7)$ _______ **14.** $25 + 5(-2)$ _______

CALCULATOR **Evaluate.**

15. $77 + 83 - 196$ _______ **16.** $67 - 13 - 12$ _______

17. $-6 \cdot 13 - 91 \div 7$ _______ **18.** $-3(-3) + 12 \div (-3)$ _______

19. $49 - [37 - (29 - 84)] - 61$ _______ **20.** $18 - 9(-4) + 105 \div (-5)$ _______

Compare. Use >, <, or =.

21. $9 + 27 \div (-9) \bigcirc -8 - 5(-2)$ **22.** $|12 - 14 - 16| \bigcirc 13 - (7 - 12)$

Insert grouping symbols to make each sentence true.

23. $8 \cdot 3 - 5 = -16$ **24.** $-30 \div 5 \times 2 = -3$

25. $8 - 7 - 6 - 5 = 0$ **26.** $-4 \cdot 8 - 3 \cdot 2 = -40$

27. $5 - 3 \div (-2) = -1$ **28.** $9 + 15 \div 8 - 20 = -17$

Solve.

29. Mark purchased four pens at $0.69 per pen. The sales tax on his purchase was $0.14. He paid for his purchase with a $10 bill. How much change did he get back? _______________

30. Find the total cost of 5 apples costing $0.23 apiece, 3 pears costing $0.32 apiece, and 6 peaches costing $0.15 apiece. _______________

31. Use the numbers 2, 4, and 6 exactly once each to write an expression equal to -2. _______________

Practice

Evaluating Expressions

Evaluate each expression for the given values of the variables.

1. $6x$ for $x = -3$ _________

2. $9 - k$ for $k = -2$ _________

3. $17 \div p$ for $p = -1$ _________

4. $|y - 8|$ for $y = 5$ _________

5. $-2 + n$ for $n = -3$ _________

6. $-m$ for $m = -1$ _________

7. $10 - r - 5$ for $r = 9$ _________

8. xy for $x = -3$, $y = -5$ _________

9. $24 - p \cdot 5$ for $p = -4$ _________

10. $5a + b$ for $a = 6$, $b = -3$ _________

11. $c + |5d|$ for $c = -10$, $d = -2$ _________

12. $m + n \div 6$ for $m = 12$, $n = -18$ _________

MENTAL MATH Evaluate each expression for the given values of
the variables.

13. $9k$ for $k = -3$ _________

14. $n - 9$ for $n = -2$ _________

15. $-7a$ for $a = 5$ _________

16. $10 - x$ for $x = -3$ _________

17. $4m + 3$ for $m = 5$ _________

18. $35 - 3x$ for $x = 10$ _________

CALCULATOR Evaluate each expression for the given values
of the variables.

19. $-178 - g$ for $g = 263$ _________

20. $1{,}221 \div (-x)$ for $x = -37$ _________

21. $p + 851$ for $p = -215$ _________

22. $7y + z$ for $y = 77$, $z = -691$ _________

23. $18a - 9b$ for $a = 12$, $b = -15$ _________

24. $-129h + k$ for $h = -17$, $k = 973$ _________

Find a value for each variable that makes the statement true.

25. $k < -7$ _____

26. $k > 17$ _____

27. $|k| = 9$ _________

28. $8k = 40$ _____

29. $-k = 15$ _____

30. $k - 9 = 12$ _____

31. $18 - k = -3$ _____

32. $2k + 5 = 19$ _____

Solve.

33. Elliot is 58 years old.

   a. Write an expression for the number of years by which

   Elliot's age exceeds that of his daughter, who is y years old. _________

   b. If his daughter is 25, how much older is Elliot? _________

34. A tree grew 27 in. each year.

   a. Write an expression for the tree's height after x years. _________

   b. When the tree is 36 years old, how tall will it be? _________

   c. A 135-in. tree is how many years old? _________

Practice

Variables and Equations

True or false?

1. $7 + 5$ is an equation. _______

2. $14 = x - 9$ is an open equation. _______

3. $8 + 7 = 10$ is an equation. _______

4. An equation is either true or false. _______

5. $-7(5 - 9) = 19 - (3)(-3)$ is a true equation. _______

If n is replaced by 7, is the equation true or false?

6. $3 - n = -4$ _______

7. $-n + 16 = 9$ _______

8. $9 = 12 - 3n$ _______

9. $3(4 + n) = 5n - 2$ _______

If the variable is replaced by the given number, is the equation true or false?

10. $-k + 15 = 6; k = 21$ _______

11. $3c + 5 = 14; c = 3$ _______

12. $-m - 4 = m; m = -2$ _______

13. $30 \div z = 11 + z, z = -5$ _______

14. $24 - 6h = h \div 4; h = 4$ _______

15. $9(4 + n) = 3n; n = -6$ _______

Is 5 a solution of each equation?

16. $x + 13 = 18$ _______

17. $8p \div (-4) = 10$ _______

18. $4 - 2y = 3(y - 7)$ _______

19. $-m - 3m = 15 - m$ _______

Is the given number a solution of the equation?

20. $9k = 10 - k, k = -1$ _______

21. $-7r - 15 = -2r; r = -3$ _______

22. $3g \div (-6) = 5 - g; g = -10$ _______

23. $(4 - 7)p = 4p + 35; p = -5$ _______

24. $8 - e = 2e - 16; e = 8$ _______

25. $5(1 - 3s) = 8 - 16s; s = 3$ _______

CALCULATOR Is the given number a solution of the equation?

26. $-19x = -741; x = 39$ _______

27. $38 - 12n = -130; n = -14$ _______

28. $816 \div (31 - p) = 12; p = -37$ _______

29. $429 + 2x = 357 - x; x = -24$ _______

MENTAL MATH Does the equation have a solution greater than zero?

30. $-6 = x + 12$ _______

31. $-24 \div x = -3$ _______

32. $t + 17 = 44$ _______

33. $7x = -35$ _______

34. $-12x + 10 = 5$ _______

35. $x \div (-1) + 1 = 0$ _______

Practice

Properties of Operations

Write the letter of the property illustrated.

1. $14(mn) = (14m)n$ _________

2. $19 + 11 = 11 + 19$ _________

3. $k \cdot 1 = k$ _________

4. $(x + y) + z = x + (y + z)$ _________

5. $65t = t(65)$ _________

6. $p = 0 + p$ _________

7. $n = 1 \cdot n$ _________

8. $(x + p) + (r + t) = (r + t) + (x + p)$ _________

9. $(h + 0) + 4 = h + 4$ _________

10. $x + yz = x + zy$ _________

    a. commutative property of addition
    b. associative property of addition
    c. commutative property of multiplication
    d. associative property of multiplication
    e. additive identity
    f. multiplicative identity

Use the commutative property to write an equivalent expression.

11. $x + 7$ _________
12. $9n$ _________
13. $h + 4$ _________

14. $-3y$ _________
15. xy _________
16. $q + r$ _________

Use the associative property to write an equivalent expression.

17. $2(9 \cdot 8)$ _________
18. $(7 + p) + 3$ _________

19. $2a(bc)$ _________
20. $x + (3 + y)$ _________

Use the multiplicative or additive identity to evaluate.

21. $8 + 0$ _________
22. $456 \cdot 1$ _________
23. $1(abc)$ _________

24. $xyz \cdot 1$ _________
25. $298q \cdot 1$ _________
26. $60mn \cdot 1$ _________

Use the commutative and associative properties to evaluate.

27. $4 \cdot 13 \cdot 25$ _________
28. $700 + 127 + 300$ _________

29. $68 + 85 + 32$ _________
30. $2 \cdot 3 \cdot 4 \cdot 5$ _________

31. $14 + 71 + 29 + 86$ _________
32. $125 \cdot 9 \cdot 8$ _________

MENTAL MATH **Evaluate.**

33. $20 \cdot 7 \cdot 5$ _________
34. $217 + 545 - 17$ _________

35. $39 + 27 + 11$ _________
36. $4 \cdot 12 \cdot 250$ _________

Practice

The Distributive Property

Write an expression for the total area.

1. 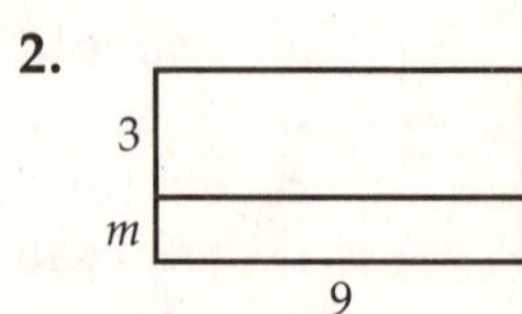

2.

3. 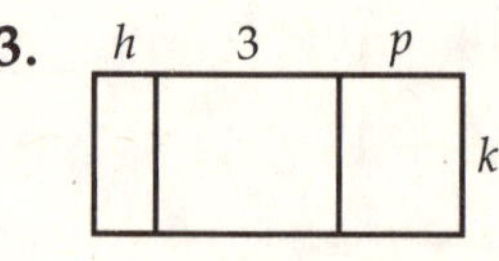

____

____

____

Write the number or variable which can be distributed.

4. $8(14 - 4)$ _________

5. $(2 + k)9$ _________

6. $(x + 3)(-5)$ _________

7. $(n - 12)h$ _________

8. $-c(m - p)$ _________

9. $(12 + 5 \div r)s$ _________

Write the number or variable which has been distributed.
Rewrite using the distributive property in reverse.

10. $8 \bullet 7 + 9 \bullet 7$ _______ ____________

11. $3 \bullet 12 - 5 \bullet 12$ _______ ____________

12. $k \bullet 15 + k(-11)$ _______ ____________

13. $x \bullet m - x \bullet n$ _______ ____________

Complete with the appropriate number or variable.

14. $12(5 + 9) = 12 \bullet 5 +$ _________ $\bullet \, 9$

15. $3 \bullet 7 - 8 \bullet 7 = ($ _________ $- 8)$ _________

16. $z(a - b - c) =$ _________ $\bullet \, a - z \bullet$ _________ $-$ _________ $\bullet$ _________

17. $[14 + (-3)]7 = 14 \bullet$ _________ $+$ _________ $\bullet \, 7$

18. $p[(-3) + n] = p \bullet$ _________ $+$ _________ $\bullet$ _________

MENTAL MATH Use the distributive property to evaluate.

19. $98 \bullet 7$ _________

20. $290 \bullet 4$ _________

21. $30 \bullet 105$ _________

22. $78 \bullet 8$ _________

23. $195 \bullet 6$ _________

24. $598 \bullet 3$ _________

25. $899 \bullet 5$ _________

26. $7 \bullet 2,009$ _________

27. $9 \bullet 28$ _________

Use the distributive property to evaluate.

28. $3(9 + 5)$ _________

29. $(8 - 12)5$ _________

30. $-4(3 + 5)$ _________

31. $3(4 + 5 + 6)$ _________

32. $6[7 + (-2)]$ _________

33. $[10 + (-3)]7$ _________

Solve using the distributive property.

34. A shipping container holds 144 boxes. How many boxes

can be shipped in 4 containers? _________

Practice

For use after 2-4 (pp. 66–69)

Simplifying Variable Expressions

Complete.

	Number of Terms	Numerical Coefficients	Like Terms
1. $3x + 7$	_____________	_____________	_____________
2. $4m + (-3n) + n$	_____________	_____________	_____________
3. $6kp + 9h + kp - 14$	_____________	_____________	_____________
4. $-8y + 6ab + 7 - 3ba$	_____________	_____________	_____________
5. $c + 2c + c - 5c + 1$	_____________	_____________	_____________

Name the property that you can use to simplify each expression.

6. $7k + (-3k)$ _____________________

7. $5x + (3x + 7)$ _____________________

8. $11(12p)$ _____________________

9. $-9y + 2y + 7$ _____________________

10. $2m - 3m - 8n + n$ _____________________

11. $2x + (x + y)$ _____________________

Combine the like terms by using the distributive property.

12. $12x - 3x$ _____________________

13. $19a + 11a$ _____________________

14. $85k + 36h + 13 - 9h$ _____________________

15. $7p + 6p + 12p - 5p$ _____________________

16. $-5a + 2a - 10 + 2$ _____________________

17. $-33 - x + 33x + 1$ _____________________

Complete with the appropriate term, number, or variable.

18. $5(n + 4) + 9n = 5 \cdot$ _________ $+$ _________ $\cdot 4 + 9n$

$\quad =$ _________ $+$ _________ $+ 9n$

$\quad = 5n + 9n + 20$

$\quad = ($ _________ $+ 9)n + 20$

$\quad =$ _________ $n + 20$

Simplify each expression.

19. $16 + 7y - 8$ _____________

20. $18m - 7 + 12m$ _____________

21. $5(3t) - 7(2t)$ _____________

22. $2x - 9y + 7x + 20y$ _____________

23. $3(9k - 4) - 4(5n - 3)$ _____________

24. $6(g - h) - 6(g - h)$ _____________

25. $-21(a + 2b) + 14a - 9b$ _____________

26. $-7a + 3(a - c) + 5c$ _____________

27. $-2(-5)q - (-72)(-q)$ _____________

28. $3(x + y) - 5x$ _____________

Practice

Addition and Subtraction Equations

Solve each equation using the subtraction property of equality.

1. $x + 14 = 21$ _____________

2. $31 = p + 17$ _____________

3. $-19 = k + 9$ _____________

4. $87 + y = 19$ _____________

5. $36 + n = 75$ _____________

6. $-176 = h + (-219)$ _____________

Solve each equation using the addition property of equality.

7. $m - 17 = -8$ _____________

8. $k - 55 = 67$ _____________

9. $-44 + n = 36$ _____________

10. $-36 = p - 91$ _____________

11. $x - 255 = 671$ _____________

12. $19 = c - (-12)$ _____________

Solve each equation using opposites.

13. $84 = z + 37$ _____________

14. $k - 55 = 23$ _____________

15. $r + 7 = -16$ _____________

16. $68 = p - 41$ _____________

17. $144 + g = 78$ _____________

18. $311 = y - 281$ _____________

MENTAL MATH Solve each equation.

19. $-52 = -52 + k$ _____________

20. $837 = p + 37$ _____________

21. $x - 155 = 15$ _____________

22. $180 = 80 + n$ _____________

23. $2{,}000 + y = 9{,}500$ _____________

24. $81 = x - 19$ _____________

25. $111 + f = 100$ _____________

26. $w - 6 = -16$ _____________

CALCULATOR Solve each equation.

27. $e + 3{,}777 = 2{,}431$ _____________

28. $45{,}709 = v - 78{,}666$ _____________

29. $145{,}719 = y + 247{,}623$ _____________

30. $m - 807{,}543 = -623{,}744$ _____________

31. $x + 558{,}399 = 845{,}919$ _____________

32. $3{,}725{,}444 = c + 4{,}210{,}500$ _____________

Solve each equation.

33. $17 + m = 21$ _____________

34. $y - 34 = 43$ _____________

35. $t + 9 = -9$ _____________

36. $15 = z + 6$ _____________

37. $41 + k = 7$ _____________

38. $1{,}523 + c = 2{,}766$ _____________

39. $-88 + z = 0$ _____________

40. $-33 + (-7) = 29 + m$ _____________

41. $t + (-2) = -66$ _____________

42. $-390 + x = 11 - 67$ _____________

Practice

Multiplication and Division Equations

Solve each equation using the division property of equality.

1. $7m = 35$ __________
2. $-3x = 18$ __________
3. $-56 = 8y$ __________
4. $90 = 10k$ __________
5. $8p = -8$ __________
6. $-4s = -32$ __________
7. $100 = -20n$ __________
8. $14h = 42$ __________
9. $-175 = 25g$ __________
10. $-87{,}654y = 0$ __________
11. $-42 = 6m$ __________
12. $-2x = 34$ __________

Solve each equation using the multiplication property of equality.

13. $\frac{b}{8} = -3$ __________
14. $\frac{k}{-5} = -5$ __________
15. $-3 = \frac{n}{7}$ __________
16. $1 = \frac{n}{14}$ __________
17. $\frac{x}{12} = 0$ __________
18. $-6 = \frac{m}{-2}$ __________
19. $\frac{p}{15} = 5$ __________
20. $\frac{y}{-4} = -12$ __________
21. $\frac{s}{30} = 6$ __________
22. $\frac{1}{4}m = -12$ __________
23. $\frac{1}{9}z = 0$ __________
24. $-\frac{m}{55} = 1$ __________

MENTAL MATH Solve each equation.

25. $\frac{w}{100} = -24$ __________
26. $50k = 500$ __________
27. $-30m = 30{,}000$ __________
28. $\frac{p}{500} = -5$ __________
29. $-40m = 4{,}000$ __________
30. $\frac{n}{60} = -6$ __________

CALCULATOR Solve each equation.

31. $511 = \frac{x}{-23}$ __________
32. $-144k = -9{,}360$ __________
33. $\frac{n}{357} = -266$ __________
34. $915y = 70{,}455$ __________
35. $58y = 12{,}006$ __________
36. $\frac{b}{473} = 68$ __________

Solve each equation using any method.

37. $54 = -18v$ __________
38. $\frac{x}{-9} = -11$ __________
39. $216 = 9w$ __________
40. $15 = \frac{k}{4}$ __________
41. $-17v = -17$ __________
42. $-161 = 23t$ __________
43. $\frac{f}{71} = 0$ __________
44. $56h = 3{,}136$ __________
45. $20 = \frac{e}{-25}$ __________
46. $-12 = \frac{j}{-3}$ __________
47. $4{,}200 = 30x$ __________
48. $\frac{y}{-21} = -21$ __________
49. $382 = 2x$ __________
50. $\frac{m}{-3} = 21$ __________
51. $4{,}000 = \frac{-x}{40}$ __________

Practice

Writing Equations

Choose the best equation for each problem. Do not solve.

1. If you were to earn \$6/h, how many hours (h) would it take you to earn \$84? _________

   a. $h + 6 = 84$ **b.** $\dfrac{h}{6} = 84$ **c.** $6h = 84$ **d.** $h = 84 - 6$

2. The quantity $k - 5$ is 4 more than -8. _________

   a. $(k - 5) + 4 = -8$ **b.** $(k - 5) - 4 = -8$

   c. $4(k - 5) = -8$ **d.** $4 - (k - 5) = -8$

Write an equation using the given variable. Do not solve.

3. Ernie scored 8 more points than Mike scored. Mike scored 16 points. How many points (p) did Ernie score?

   ____

4. One-fifth of a number (n) is equal to -7. _________

5. A bamboo tree grew 3 in. per day. How many days (d) did it take the tree to grow 144 in.?

   ____

6. A truck driver drove 468 miles on Tuesday. That was 132 miles farther than she drove on Monday. How far (d) did she drive on Monday?

   ____

Write an equation for each problem. Then solve.

7. The product of a number and -7 is -91.

   Equation _______________________ Solution _________

8. Carl's car averages 33 miles per gallon of gas. How much gas will he use driving 561 miles?

   Equation _______________________ Solution _________

9. The combined enrollment in the three grades at Jefferson Middle School is 977. There are 356 students in the seventh grade and 365 in the eighth grade. How many students are there in the ninth grade?

   Equation _______________________ Solution _________

■■■ **Practice**

Guess and Test

Use guess and test to solve each problem.

1. The length of a rectangle is 9 in. greater than the width. The area is 36 in.^{2} Find the dimensions. ___________________________________

2. Michael Jordan scored 30 points on 2-point and 3-point goals. He hit 5 more 2-pointers than 3-pointers. How many of each did he score? ___________________________________

3. The sums and products of pairs of integers are given. Find each pair of integers.

   a. sum = -12, product = 36 __________

   b. sum = -12, product = 35 __________

   c. sum = -12, product = 32 __________

   d. sum = -12, product = 11 __________

   e. sum = -12, product = 0 __________

4. Jess had 3 more nickels than dimes for a total of $1.50. How many of each coin did he have?

   ____

5. A brush cost $2 more than a comb. The brush and a comb together cost $3.78. Find the cost of each.

   ____

6. The hard-cover edition of a book costs 3 times as much as the paperback edition. Both editions together cost $26.60. Find the cost of each.

   ____

7. The Wolverines scored 42 points in a football game. They scored 2 more field goals (3 points each) than touchdowns (6 points each). How many field goals and touchdowns did they score?

   ____

8. The volume of a box is equal to the product of the length, width, and height ($V = lwh$). The height and width of a shoe box are equal. The height is 6 in. less than the length. The volume of the box is 896 in.^{3} Find the length, width, and height of the box.

   ____

Practice

For use after 3-1 (pp. 100–103)

Decimals

Write each decimal in words.

1. 7.316 ____

2. 504.07 ____

3. 0.20008 ____

4. Graph each decimal on the number line. Write the letter above the point.

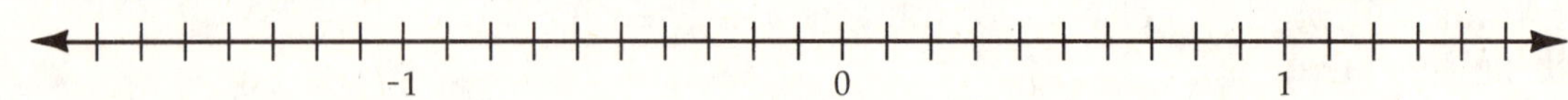

A. −1.3   **B.** 0.7   **C.** |−1.1| **D.** −0.3   **E.** −1.55   **F.** −0.85

Compare. Write >, <, or =.

5. −2.1 ☐ 1.4 **6.** 5.3 ☐ 5.33 **7.** −3 ☐ −3.0

8. 9.80 ☐ 9.08 **9.** −6.1 ☐ −6.01 **10.** −8.336 ☐ −8.363

11. 17.5 ☐ 17.50 **12.** −0.03 ☐ −0.003 **13.** 7.001 ☐ 7.0001

Order from greatest to least.

14. 3.7, 3.07, 3.077 ___________________ **15.** −1.9, −1.99, −1.09 ___________________

16. 0.06, 0.006, 0.60, 0.66 ____

17. −8.014, −8.0041, −8.401, −8.104 ______________________________________

Write a decimal between the given decimals.

18. 0 and 0.1 __________ **19.** 8.7 and 8.8 __________

20. −0.3 and −0.2 __________ **21.** −1.44 and −1.43 __________

Round each decimal to the indicated place.

22. 0.5339, nearest hundredth __________ **23.** −2.665, nearest tenth __________

24. 2.4051, nearest hundredth __________ **25.** −0.9996, nearest thousandth __________

26. Order from fastest to slowest the winning speeds of the Olympic men's downhill skiing event. _______________________________

____

____

Year	Time
1964	2 min 18.16 s
1968	1 min 59.85 s
1972	1 min 51.43 s
1976	1 min 45.73 s
1980	1 min 45.50 s
1984	1 min 45.59 s

  Chapter 3

Practice

Estimating with Decimals

Estimate how much of each region is shaded. Use decimal numbers.

1.  ________

2.  ________

3. 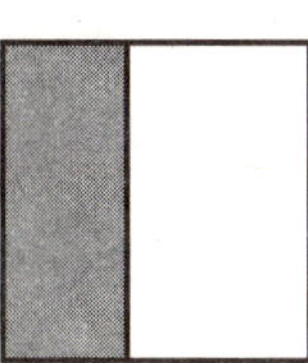 ________

Estimate using rounding.

4. 14.66 + 25.19 ________

5. 8.7 + 3.21 + 3.899 ________

6. 194.78 − 12.31 ________

7. 1.88(8.13) ________

8. 80.4 ÷ 19.72 ________

9. 36.19 + 18.4 + 23.85 + 11.9 ________

10. 29.571 • 20.44 ________

11. 507.639 ÷ 9.84 ________

Estimate using front-end estimation.

12. 6.3 + 8.55 + 4.09 ________

13. 34 + 68 + 85 ________

14. 460 + 553 + 789 ________

15. $6.14 + $9.38 + $2.53 ________

16. $39.65 + $25.84 + $11.45 ________

17. 19.71 + 3.94 + 8.4 ________

Estimate using compatible numbers.

18. 11.57 ÷ 3.09 ________

19. 43.68 ÷ 8.7 ________

20. 29.5 ÷ 5.1 ________

21. $41.09 ÷ $6.88 ________

22. 148.8 ÷ 9.8 ________

23. $76.77 ÷ $24.19 ________

Estimate using the technique which seems best.

24. 6.3 + 8.7 + 24.8 + 10.2 ________

25. 3.8(7.9) ________

26. 85.7 + 19.66 ________

27. 15.831 ÷ 7.87 ________

28. 521.063 − 25.19 ________

29. $49.65 • 19.7 ________

30. 18.75 + (−14.33) + 36.5 + 21.31 + (−5.81) ________

Use estimation to place the decimal point in each answer.

31. 62.77(29.8) = 1 8 7 0 5 4 6

32. 16.132 ÷ 2.96 = 5 4 5

33. 85.2 + 39.6 + 14.97 = 1 3 9 7 7

34. Apples cost $.89 per lb. Estimate the cost of three 5-lb bags. ________

■ *Practice*

Expressions with Decimals

Find the value of $38 - 0.6n$ for the given value of n.

1. $n = 5$ _________   **2.** $n = 4.2$ _________   **3.** $n = 52$ _________

Evaluate each expression for $h = 8.5$.

4. $-7.4h$ _________   **5.** $31.97 + h$ _________

6. $-9.4 - h$ _________   **7.** $84.15 \div h$ _________

Evaluate each expression for $x = 4.37$ and $y = -2.9$.

8. $x + y$ _________   **9.** $x - y$ _________

10. $-x + 8.55$ _________   **11.** $2y + 3x$ _________

12. $-4y - 17.9$ _________   **13.** $2.2(y - x)$ _________

14. $\dfrac{2x + 0.36}{5}$ _________   **15.** $\dfrac{2x + y}{-0.73}$ _________

16. $\dfrac{4 - y}{x + 18.63}$ _________   **17.** $x(1 - 8y)$ _________

MENTAL MATH Evaluate each expression.

18. $-10m$ for $m = 7.381$ _________   **19.** $e + f$ for $e = 8.7$ and $f = -3.7$ _________

20. $0.01k$ for $k = 2{,}371.6$ _________   **21.** $5p$ for $p = -3.07$ _________

CALCULATOR Evaluate each expression.

22. $\dfrac{45.549}{x}$ for $x = -7.23$ _________   **23.** $-0.84x$ for $x = -1.23$ _________

24. $6.2x - 3.9y$ for $x = -0.07$ and $y = 1.4$ _________

25. $x - y - x(32 - 5y)$ for $x = 3.4$ and $y = 2.52$ _________

Simplify.

26. $19.4 \cdot 7.7x$ _________   **27.** $6.154x \div 1.81$ _________

28. $9.85(4.71x) \div 1.97$ _________   **29.** $44.73x - 72.19x$ _________

ESTIMATION Estimate the value if $x = 17.82$ and $y = 3.17$.

30. $x + y$ _________   **31.** $x - 3y$ _________

32. $x \div 2y$ _________   **33.** $40 - 2x$ _________

Solve.

34. The total cost, including tax, of an item selling for x dollars

     is $1.05x$. Find the total cost of a chair that sells for \$240. _________

          Chapter 3

Practice

Addition and Subtraction Equations

Solve each equation using the subtraction property of equality.

1. $9.36 + k = 14.8$ _______________

2. $-22 = p + 13.7$ _______________

3. $y + 3.85 = 2.46$ _______________

4. $-13.8 = h + 15.603$ _______________

Solve each equation using opposites.

5. $x + 82.7 = 63.5$ _______________

6. $-0.08 = f + 0.07$ _______________

7. $0 = a + 27.98$ _______________

8. $117.345 + m = 200$ _______________

Solve each equation using the addition property of equality.

9. $3.8 = n - 3.62$ _______________

10. $x - 19.7 = -17.48$ _______________

11. $12.5 = t - 3.55$ _______________

12. $k - 263.48 = -381.09$ _______________

Solve each equation using opposites.

13. $y - 48.763 = 0$ _______________

14. $6.21 = e + (-3.48)$ _______________

15. $x + (-0.0025) = 0.0024$ _______________

16. $-58.109 = v - 47.736$ _______________

MENTAL MATH **Solve each equation.**

17. $k + 23.7 = 23.7$ _______________

18. $5.63 = n + 1.63$ _______________

19. $x - 3.2 = 4.1$ _______________

20. $p - 0.7 = 9.3$ _______________

CALCULATOR **Solve each equation.**

21. $-8.557 + y = 17.498$

____

22. $265.89 = n - 188.775$

____

23. $k - 0.88425 = 3.7429$

____

24. $298{,}416.7 + p = -377{,}598.86$

____

Solve each equation using any method.

25. $n - 17.9 = -31.05$ _______________

26. $4{,}365.77 = c + 7{,}935.49$ _______________

27. $4.4 = p + 1.1$ _______________

28. $k + (-8.5) = -0.6$ _______________

29. $t + 18.5 = -41$ _______________

30. $y - 33.4 = 81.9$ _______________

31. $-15.7 = k + 20.4$ _______________

32. $h - 215.876 = -114.015$ _______________

33. $z - 81.6 = -81.6$ _______________

34. $5.4 = t + (-6.1)$ _______________

35. $-4.095 + b = 18.665$ _______________

36. $4.87 = n + 0.87$ _______________

Practice

For use after 3-5 (pp. 115–118)

Multiplication and Division Equations

Solve using the division property of equality.

1. $-9k = 2.34$ _____________

2. $-12.42 = 0.03p$ _____________

3. $-7.2y = 61.2$ _____________

4. $-0.1035 = 0.23n$ _____________

5. $1.5m = 3.03$ _____________

6. $-0.007h = 0.2002$ _____________

7. $8.13t = -100.812$ _____________

8. $0.546 = 0.42y$ _____________

Solve using the multiplication property of equality.

9. $\frac{p}{2.9} = 0.55$ _____________

10. $9.1 = \frac{x}{-0.7}$ _____________

11. $-6.4 = \frac{y}{8.5}$ _____________

12. $\frac{k}{-1.2} = -0.07$ _____________

13. $277.4 = \frac{n}{3.5}$ _____________

14. $\frac{e}{-0.76} = 2{,}809$ _____________

15. $\frac{a}{27} = -32.3$ _____________

16. $\frac{p}{-1.52} = -3{,}600$ _____________

MENTAL MATH Solve each equation.

17. $0.7h = 4.2$ _____________

18. $\frac{x}{2.5} = -3$ _____________

19. $38.7 = -100k$ _____________

20. $-45.6e = -4.56$ _____________

CALCULATOR Solve each equation. Round each answer to the nearest hundredth.

21. $-3.77p = 19.84$ _____________

22. $\frac{k}{0.852} = -91.76$ _____________

23. $0.0046 = 0.0041x$ _____________

24. $417.92c = 316.55$ _____________

25. $-2{,}885.9 = 0.32y$ _____________

26. $-55.7 = \frac{z}{-83.6}$ _____________

27. $\frac{x}{3.04} = 3.04$ _____________

28. $\frac{-x}{-27.3} = 0.98$ _____________

Write an equation for each sentence. Solve.

29. The opposite of seventy-five hundredths times some number equals twenty-four thousandths.

   ____

30. A number divided by -3.88 equals negative two thousand.

   ____

31. Four hundredths times some number equals thirty-three and four tenths.

   ____

Chapter 3

Practice

Using Formulas

Use the formula $C = 3.14d$ to approximate the circumference of the circle where C is the circumference and d is the diameter.

1. $d = 18$ in. _______________

2. $d = 12.4$ cm _______________

3. $d = 224.5$ cm _______________

4. $d = 0.06$ km _______________

Use the formula $A = 180 - (B + C)$ to find the measure of angle A where A, B, and C are the measures of angles A, B, and C of $\triangle ABC$.

5. $B = 27°$, $C = 95°$ _______________

6. $B = 110.6°$, $C = 29.8°$ _______________

7. $B = 0.85°$, $C = 3.44°$ _______________

8. $B = 144.32°$, $C = 16.99°$ _______________

Use the formula $V = lwh$ to find the volume of the rectangular prism where V is the volume, l is the length, w is the width, and h is the height.

9. $l = 38$ in., $w = 14.25$ in., $h = 19.5$ in. _______________

10. $l = 8.4$ cm, $w = 6.4$ cm, $h = 3.2$ cm _______________

Use the formula $S = 6.28r(r + h)$ to approximate the surface area of the cylinder where S is the surface area, r is the radius, and h is the height.

11. $r = 3.8$ cm, $h = 10.2$ cm _______________

12. $r = 0.46$ m, $h = 0.85$ m _______________

Use the formula $E = \frac{9r}{I}$ and the table to find each pitcher's earned run average where E is the earned run average, r is the number of runs, and I is the number of innings pitched. Round answers to the nearest hundredth.

Pitcher	Innings	Runs
Marichal	300	70
Seaver	286	56
Ryan	149	28
Blue	312	63
Hunter	318	88
Clemens	254	70

13. Marichal _______

14. Seaver _______

15. Ryan _______

16. Blue _______

17. Hunter _______

18. Clemens _______

19. Rank the pitchers in order from lowest earned run average to highest.

____

Use the formula $I = Prt$ to find the amount of interest where I is interest, P is principal, r is rate, and t is time.

20. $P = \$800$, $r = 0.06$, $t = 3$ _______

21. $P = \$2,400$, $r = 0.085$, $t = 2.5$ _______

Practice

Simplify the Problem

Solve by using simpler problems.

1. At the inauguration, the President was honored with a 21-gun salute. The report from each gunshot lasted 1 s. Four seconds elapsed between shots. How long did the salute last?

    ____

2. Bernie began building a model airplane on day 7 of his summer vacation and finished building it on day 65. He worked on the plane each day. How many days did it take?

    ____

3. A house-number manufacturer sold numbers to retail stores for $.09 per digit. A hardware store bought enough digits for two of every house number from 1 to 999. How many digits did the store purchase for house numbers:

    a. 1–9 _____________   **b.** 10–99 _____________   **c.** 100–999 _____________

    d. Find the total cost of the house numbers. _____________

4. A tic-tac-toe diagram uses 2 vertical lines and 2 horizontal lines to create 9 spaces. How many spaces can you create using:

    a. 1 vertical line and 1 horizontal line _________

    b. 2 vertical lines and 1 horizontal line _________

    c. 3 vertical lines and 3 horizontal lines _________

    d. 4 vertical lines and 5 horizontal lines _________

    e. 17 vertical lines and 29 horizontal lines _________

5. Each side of each triangle in the figures has length 1 cm. The perimeter (the distance around) the first triangle is 3 cm. Find the perimeter of the figure formed by connecting:

     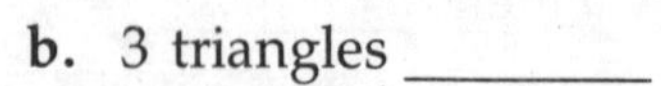

    a. 2 triangles _________   **b.** 3 triangles _________

    c. 4 triangles _________   **d.** 50 triangles _________

Practice

For use after 4-1 (pp. 141–144)

Exponents

Write using exponents.

1. $3 \cdot 3 \cdot 3 \cdot 3$ _____________

2. $k \cdot k \cdot k \cdot k \cdot k$ _____________

3. $(-9)(-9)(-9)m \cdot m \cdot m$ _____________

4. $g \cdot g \cdot g \cdot g \cdot h$ _____________

5. $7 \cdot a \cdot a \cdot b \cdot b \cdot b$ _____________

6. $2 \cdot 2 \cdot 2 \cdot 2 \cdot 2 \cdot 2 \cdot 2$ _____________

7. $\underbrace{15 \cdot 15 \cdot 15 \cdot \ldots \cdot 15}_{25 \text{ factors}}$ _____________

8. $\underbrace{x \cdot x \cdot x \cdot x \cdot \ldots \cdot x}_{e \text{ factors}}$ _____________

9. $(5m)(5m)(5m)(5m)(5m)$ _____________

10. $(y - 3z)(y - 3z)(y - 3z)(y - 3z)$ _____________

Evaluate.

11. 2^5 _________ 12. 6^3 _________ 13. 3^4 _________

14. 1^{10} _________ 15. 10^5 _________ 16. 0^{12} _________

17. $(-1)^9$ _________ 18. $(-2)^3$ _________ 19. -2^3 _________

20. m^4 for $m = 4$ _________ 21. $(5a)^3$ for $a = -1$ _________

22. $-(2p)^2$ for $p = 7$ _________ 23. $-n^6$ for $n = 2$ _________

24. b^6 for $b = -1$ _________ 25. $(e - 2)^3$ for $e = 11$ _________

CALCULATOR **Use a calculator to find the square root.**

26. $\sqrt{256}$ _________ 27. $\sqrt{400}$ _________

28. $\sqrt{121}$ _________ 29. $\sqrt{225}$ _________

30. $\sqrt{144}$ _________ 31. $\sqrt{576}$ _________

32. $\sqrt{900}$ _________ 33. $\sqrt{324}$ _________

34. $\sqrt{1,600}$ _________ 35. $\sqrt{529}$ _________

Compare. Use <, >, or =.

36. 3^2 _________ 2^3 37. 4^3 _________ 5^2

38. $2 \cdot 3^2$ _________ $3 \cdot 2^2$ 39. 4^4 _________ 5^5

40. -2^3 _________ 2^3 41. $(-3)^2$ _________ -3^2

42. 10^2 _________ 2^{10} 43. 2543^0 _________ 1^{310}

44. 8^1 _________ 2^3 45. -8^1 _________ -2^3

46. $(-1)^5$ _________ 1^5 47. -1^5 _________ 1^5

48. **MENTAL MATH** Given that $3^5 = 243$, find 3^6 mentally. _________

Practice

For use after 4-2 (pp. 145–148)

Rules About Exponents

Evaluate. No variable has a value of zero.

1. $(-5)^2$ _________
2. -5^2 _________
3. $-(5^2)$ _________
4. $(x^3)(x^4)$ _________
5. $(x^4)(y^2)(x^2)$ _________
6. $3x^2 \cdot 2x^3$ _________
7. $y^4 \cdot y^5$ _________
8. $(2^4)(4^2)$ _________
9. $(4^3)(3^4)$ _________
10. $(-y^5)(y^2)$ _________
11. $(x^3)(-x^2)$ _________
12. $(z^3)^5$ _________
13. $(3y^2)(2y^3)$ _________
14. $-(m^4)^3$ _________
15. $(-m^4)^3$ _________

Evaluate each expression for $a = 2$, $b = -1$, and $c = 4$.

16. $(ab)^2$ _________
17. $(c^2)^2$ _________
18. $(2a)^3$ _________
19. a^5b^{10} _________
20. $(b + c)^3$ _________
21. a^3c^2 _________
22. a^4b^4 _________
23. $a^3 + c^2$ _________
24. $a^4b^2c^0$ _________

True or False?

25. $y^2 \cdot x^3 = (xy)^5$ _________
26. $4^6 = 6^4$ _________
27. $z^2 \cdot z^6 = z^3 \cdot z^4$ _________

Is the given expression equal to 3^{12}? Write yes or no.

28. $(3^3)^4$ _________
29. $3^6 + 3^6$ _________
30. $3^4 \cdot 3^3$ _________
31. $3^9 \cdot 3^3$ _________

Is the value of the given expression three times the value of 3^8?
Write yes or no.

32. 3^{24} _________
33. $3 \cdot 3^8$ _________
34. $19{,}683$ _________
35. 3^{11} _________

Compare. Use >, <, or =.

36. $(4^3)^2$ _________ $(4^2)^3$
37. $5^3 \cdot 5^4$ _________ 5^{10}
38. $(3^5)^4$ _________ 3^{10}
39. 25^0 _________ 5^2
40. $(3^{12})^0$ _________ $(12^3)^0$
41. $4^2 \cdot 4^3$ _________ 4^5
42. $(6^2)^0$ _________ 6^0
43. $5^0 \cdot 5^6$ _________ 5^7
44. $(8^3)^2$ _________ $(8^2)^3$

Chapter 4

Practice

Scientific Notation

Write each number in scientific notation.

1. Pluto is about 3,653,000,000 mi from the sun. _____________

2. There are 63,360 in. in a mile. _____________

3. At its closest, Mercury is about 46,000,000 km from the sun. _____________

4. 77,250,000 _____________

5. 526,000 _____________

6. 8 billion _____________

7. 26 _____________

8. 745 million _____________

9. 8,100,000,000 _____________

10. 888,200,000 _____________

11. 5,700 _____________

Write each number in standard notation.

12. 10^4 _____________

13. 10^6 _____________

14. 3.77×10^4 _____________

15. 8.5×10^3 _____________

16. 9.002×10^5 _____________

17. 1.91×10^5 _____________

18. 5.32×10^7 _____________

19. 3.21×10^9 _____________

20. 8.002×10^2 _____________

21. 4.6×10^3 _____________

Simplify. Write each number in scientific notation. Round to the nearest tenth. Then write the rounded number in standard notation.

	Scientific	Standard
22. $(2 \times 10^5)(3 \times 10^2)$		
23. $(1.665 \times 10^6) \div (3.7 \times 10^4)$		
24. $72,000 \times 143,000$		
25. $(1.5 \times 10^5)(4 \times 10^9)$		
26. $(3.2 \times 10^6)(5.1 \times 10^3)$		
27. $9,400(2.5 \times 10^5)$		

Complete.

28. $62.4 = $ _________ $\times 10^1$

29. $6.24 = 6.24 \times 10 \text{———}$

30. $62,400 = 6.24 \times 10 \text{———}$

31. _________ $= 6.24 \times 10^2$

Practice

Factors, Multiples, and Divisibility

**Decide whether the first number is a factor of the second.
Write yes or no.**

1. 6; 54 _________

2. 4; 76 _________

3. 3; 107 _________

4. 5; 424 _________

5. 10; 6,270 _________

6. 9; 711 _________

7. 3; 555 _________

8. 6; 566 _________

9. 12; 504 _________

10. 9; 251,613 _________

11. 5; 13,360 _________

12. 4; 428 _________

List all the factors of each number.

13. 12 _______________________________

14. 35 _______________________________

15. 41 _______________________________

16. 54 _______________________________

List the first five multiples of each number.

17. 3 _______________________________

18. 7 _______________________________

19. 18 _______________________________

20. 35 _______________________________

**Decide whether each number is divisible by 2, 3, 5, or 9. Write
yes or no for each divisor.**

21. 215 _______________________________

22. 432 _______________________________

23. 770 _______________________________

24. 1,011 _______________________________

25. 975 _______________________________

26. 2,070 _______________________________

27. 3,707 _______________________________

28. 5,715 _______________________________

Write the missing digit to make each number divisible by 9.

29. 7 ☐ 1

30. 2,2 ☐ 2

31. 88 ☐ 12

32. There are four different digits which, when inserted in the
blank space in the number 4 ☐ 5, make the number divisible
by 3. Write them. _______________

33. There are two different digits which, when inserted in the
blank space in the number 7,16 ☐ , make the number
divisible by 5. Write them. _______________

34. There are five different digits which, when inserted in the
blank space in the number 99,99 ☐ , make the number
divisible by 2. Write them. _______________

Practice

Prime Factorization

Tell whether each number is prime or composite. Write *p* or *c*.

1. 19 ___   **2.** 38 ___   **3.** 57 ___   **4.** 83 ___

5. 171 ___   **6.** 365 ___   **7.** 137 ___   **8.** 543 ___

Write the prime factorization using division.

9. 75 ___________   **10.** 152 ___________   **11.** 143 ___________

12. 432 ___________   **13.** 588 ___________   **14.** 369 ___________

Write the prime factorization using a factor tree.

15. 160 ___________   **16.** 108 ___________   **17.** 531 ___________

CALCULATOR Find the number with the given prime factorization.

18. $3^2 \cdot 5^3 \cdot 7$ ___________   **19.** 11^3 ___________   **20.** $7^2 \cdot 13^2$ ___________

21. $2^5 \cdot 3 \cdot 13$ ___________   **22.** $13 \cdot 29 \cdot 43$ ___________   **23.** $2^3 \cdot 7 \cdot 11 \cdot 17$ ___________

24. $2^5 \cdot 3^4 \cdot 5^1$ ___________   **25.** 7^4 ___________   **26.** $7 \cdot 11^2$ ___________

ESTIMATION Use the numbers 7, 11, 17, and 23 to find the prime factors.

27. 187 ___________   **28.** 161 ___________   **29.** 539 ___________

30. 391 ___________   **31.** 3,703 ___________   **32.** 2,401 ___________

Solve.

33. The numbers 3, 5, and 7 are factors of n. Find four other factors of n.

____

34. Both a and b are odd whole numbers. Is $2ab - 1$ even or odd? Explain.

____

35. Both m and n are prime numbers. Is $m \times n$ prime? Explain.

____

Practice

GCF and LCM

Find the GCF of each set.

1. 8, 12 _________
2. 36, 54 _________
3. 63, 81 _________
4. 69, 92 _________
5. 15, 28 _________
6. 21, 35 _________
7. $30m$, $36n$ _________
8. $75x^3y^2$, $100xy$ _________
9. 15, 24, 30 _________
10. 48, 80, 128 _________
11. $36hk^3$, $60k^2m$, $84k^4n$ _________
12. $2mn$, $4m^2n^2$ _________

Find the LCM of each set.

13. 6, 8 _________
14. 10, 12 _________
15. 13, 15 _________
16. 7, 21 _________
17. 24, 32 _________
18. 15, 50 _________
19. $9a^3b$, $18abc$ _________
20. $28xy^2$, $42x^2y$ _________
21. 3, 4, 5 _________
22. 9, 12, 16 _________
23. $6m^3$, $14mp^4$, $21mp^2$ _________
24. $10x^2y$, $100x^5y^7z$, $5z$ _________
25. $2mn$, $26m^7n^3$, $8mn^{10}$ _________

CALCULATOR **Find the GCF and LCM for each set of numbers.**

26. 192, 288 GCF _________ LCM _________
27. 133, 551 GCF _________ LCM _________
28. 138, 368, 828 GCF _________ LCM _________

Solve.

29. A quality control inspector in an egg factory checks every forty-eighth egg for cracks and every fifty-fourth egg for weight. What is the number of the first egg each day that the inspector checks for both qualities?

    ____

30. The numbers m and n are both prime numbers.

    a. What is the GCF of m and n? _________

    b. What is the LCM of m and n? _________

31. The LCM of 24 and x is 888. What is the LCM of 8, 24, and x?

    ____

32. The GCF of a and b is 15. What is the GCF of a, b, and 5?

    ____

Practice

Account for All Possibilities

Solve by accounting systematically for all possibilities.

1. A baseball team has 4 pitchers and 3 catchers. How many different pitcher-catcher combinations are possible?

   ____

2. The baseball team has 2 first basemen, 3 second basemen, and 2 third basemen. How many combinations of the three positions are possible?

   ____

3. A quarter is tossed 3 times. In how many different orders can heads and tails be tossed?

   ____

4. A quarter is tossed 4 times. In how many different orders can heads and tails be tossed?

   ____

5. Curtains are manufactured in 3 different styles and 5 different colors.

   a. How many different style-color combinations are possible?

   ____

   b. The curtains are produced in 2 different fabrics. How many different style-color-fabric combinations are possible?

   ____

6. A vending machine accepts any combination of nickels, dimes, and quarters equaling 50¢. How many combinations of coins are possible?

   ____

7. Joe remembered that the three digits in his locker combination were 3, 5, and 7, but he forgot the order of the numbers. What is the maximum number of combinations he must check in order to open his lock?

   ____

8. The first digit of a 3-digit telephone area code is 6 or 7. The second digit is 9. How many codes are possible?

   ____

Practice

Equivalent Fractions and Lowest Terms

Write a fraction for each sentence.

1. Montana completed 18 passes in 29 attempts. ___________

2. One of the 12 light bulbs was defective. ___________

Complete the chart.

Model	Word name	Fraction
3. ●●○○○○	one-third	___________
4. ■■■■■□□□□□	___________	$\frac{1}{2}$
5. △△△△△	___________	___________

Write a fraction for each shaded region.

6. 

7. 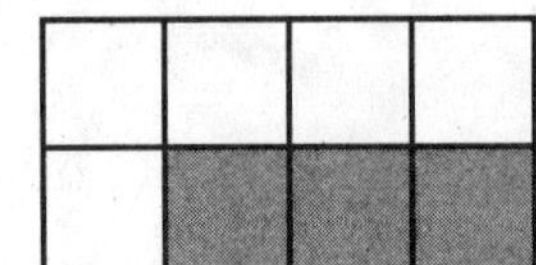

8. 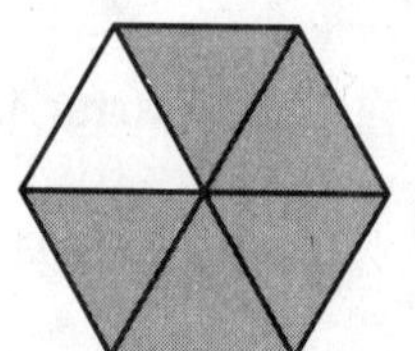

_______   _______   _______

Write three fractions equivalent to each fraction.

9. $\frac{1}{4}$ _______ _______ _______   10. $\frac{2}{3}$ _______ _______ _______

11. $\frac{3}{5}$ _______ _______ _______   12. $\frac{3}{18}$ _______ _______ _______

13. $\frac{8k}{16k}$ _______ _______ _______   14. $\frac{3m}{8n}$ _______ _______ _______

MENTAL MATH **Rename the variable to form equivalent fractions.**

15. $\frac{1}{2} = \frac{6}{n}$ _______   16. $\frac{2}{5} = \frac{m}{20}$ _______   17. $\frac{9}{21} = \frac{3}{x}$ _______

18. $\frac{e}{10} = \frac{12}{40}$ _______   19. $\frac{5}{6} = \frac{15}{x}$ _______   20. $\frac{21}{c} = \frac{7}{8}$ _______

Write in lowest terms.

21. $\frac{10}{15}$ _______   22. $\frac{18}{36}$ _______   23. $\frac{27}{36}$ _______   24. $\frac{12}{15}$ _______

25. $\frac{6xy}{16y}$ _______   26. $\frac{24n^2}{28n}$ _______   27. $\frac{30hxy}{54kxy}$ _______   28. $\frac{16y^3}{20y^4}$ _______

Practice

Fractions and Decimals

Use each model to answer the questions.

1. △ △ △ △
   △ △ △

   a. Let each piece represent $\frac{1}{5}$. What improper fraction is shown?

   ____

   b. What mixed number is shown?

   ____

   c. What decimal is shown?

   ____

2. ☐ ☐ ☐
   ☐ ☐

   a. Let each piece represent $\frac{1}{2}$. What improper fraction is shown?

   ____

   b. What mixed number is shown?

   ____

   c. What decimal is shown?

   ____

Write each mixed number as an improper fraction.

3. $2\frac{2}{3}$ _______   4. $4\frac{3}{5}$ _______   5. $1\frac{6}{7}$ _______   6. $5\frac{1}{2}$ _______

7. $6\frac{5}{8}$ _______   8. $2\frac{7}{11}$ _______   9. $3\frac{1}{9}$ _______   10. $8\frac{3}{4}$ _______

Write each improper fraction as a mixed number.

11. $\frac{10}{3}$ _______   12. $\frac{17}{5}$ _______   13. $\frac{29}{4}$ _______   14. $\frac{39}{7}$ _______

15. $\frac{40}{9}$ _______   16. $\frac{53}{6}$ _______   17. $\frac{81}{10}$ _______   18. $\frac{109}{15}$ _______

Write each decimal as a mixed number or fraction in lowest terms.

19. 0.4 _______   20. 0.75 _______   21. 0.16 _______   22. 1.95 _______

23. 2.34 _______   24. 0.09 _______   25. 8.8 _______   26. 5.008 _______

CALCULATOR Write as a decimal.

27. $\frac{17}{20}$ _______   28. $\frac{7}{8}$ _______   29. $\frac{9}{16}$ _______   30. $\frac{13}{25}$ _______

31. $3\frac{1}{8}$ _______   32. $6\frac{9}{32}$ _______   33. $2\frac{87}{125}$ _______   34. $4\frac{31}{50}$ _______

35. Write an improper fraction with the greatest possible value using each of the digits 5, 7, and 9 once. Write this as a mixed number and as a decimal.

____

Practice

Rational Numbers

Write a rational number to represent each situation.

1. the number of years in 30 months ____________

2. the number of yards in 14 ft ____________

Write a rational number for each point on the number line.

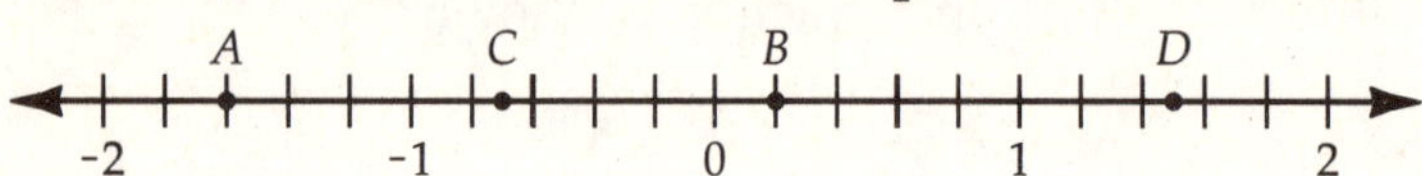

3. A ________   4. B ________   5. C ________   6. D ________

Graph each point on the number line. Write the letter above the point.

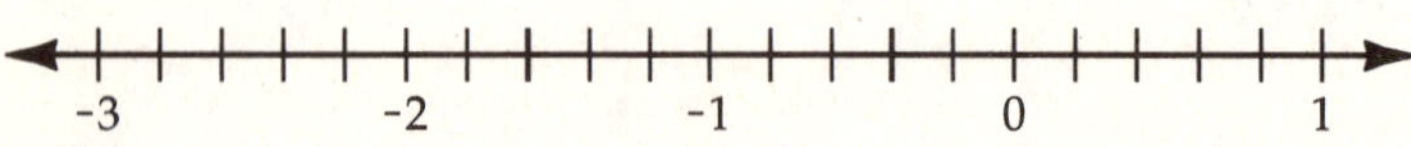

7. E: $-\frac{4}{5}$ 8. F: $-2\frac{1}{2}$ 9. G: 0.4 10. H: -1.9

Write the opposite and the absolute value.

11. -5.61 ________ ________   12. $3\frac{5}{8}$ ________ ________

13. $-\frac{11}{3}$ ________ ________   14. 0.78 ________ ________

15. Which rational numbers are equal to $-\frac{17}{10}$? ________

    a. -17 **b.** -1.7 **c.** $-\frac{34}{20}$ **d.** 0.17

16. Which rational numbers are equal to $\frac{3}{5}$? ________

    a. $\frac{12}{20}$ **b.** $\frac{-3}{-5}$ **c.** 0.3 **d.** 0.6

17. Which rational numbers are equal to $\frac{12}{15}$? ________

    a. $\frac{4}{5}$ **b.** 0.05 **c.** 0.95 **d.** 0.8

Evaluate. Write in lowest terms.

18. $\frac{x}{y}$ for $x = 12$, $y = 21$ ________   19. $\frac{n}{n+p}$ for $n = 9$, $p = 6$ ________

20. $\frac{k}{k^2+4}$ for $k = 6$ ________   21. $\frac{x^2+2x+1}{x+1}$ for $x = 5$ ________

Write each rational expression in lowest terms.

22. $\frac{8x}{10y}$ ________   23. $\frac{3 \cdot 7 \cdot n^2}{6 \cdot 21 \cdot n}$ ________   24. $\frac{12h^3k}{16h^2k^2}$ ________

25. $\frac{abc}{10abc}$ ________   26. $\frac{mn^2}{pm^5n}$ ________   27. $\frac{5jh}{15jh^3}$ ________

Practice

Comparing and Ordering Rational Numbers

Compare. Use >, <, or =.

1. $\frac{2}{3} \bigcirc \frac{7}{9}$
2. $\frac{3}{5} \bigcirc \frac{7}{10}$
3. $-\frac{3}{4} \bigcirc -\frac{13}{16}$

4. $\frac{9}{21} \bigcirc \frac{6}{14}$
5. $-\frac{2}{8} \bigcirc -\frac{7}{32}$
6. $\frac{7}{9} \bigcirc -\frac{8}{9}$

7. $\frac{5}{8} \bigcirc \frac{7}{12}$
8. $-\frac{4}{5} \bigcirc -\frac{7}{8}$
9. $-\frac{4}{18} \bigcirc -\frac{6}{27}$

10. $-\frac{5}{18} \bigcirc -\frac{2}{9}$
11. $\frac{7}{12} \bigcirc \frac{11}{18}$
12. $\frac{13}{20} \bigcirc \frac{11}{15}$

13. $-\frac{11}{20} \bigcirc -\frac{22}{40}$
14. $\frac{6}{5} \bigcirc \frac{1}{5}$
15. $\frac{11}{28} \bigcirc \frac{14}{19}$

MENTAL MATH **Compare. Use >, <, or =.**

16. $\frac{8}{17} \bigcirc -\frac{3}{8}$
17. $-\frac{7}{6} \bigcirc -\frac{6}{7}$
18. $\frac{-9}{-11} \bigcirc \frac{9}{11}$

19. $\frac{1}{3} \bigcirc -\frac{3}{9}$
20. $-\frac{12}{6} \bigcirc -\frac{9}{3}$
21. $\frac{5}{10} \bigcirc \frac{3}{4}$

22. $\frac{7}{11} \bigcirc -\frac{9}{10}$
23. $-\frac{2}{4} \bigcirc -\frac{5}{8}$
24. $\frac{5}{12} \bigcirc \frac{3}{10}$

CALCULATOR **Compare. Use >, <, or =.**

25. $\frac{5}{6} \bigcirc \frac{9}{11}$
26. $-\frac{11}{17} \bigcirc -\frac{17}{24}$
27. $\frac{21}{29} \bigcirc \frac{24}{33}$

28. $-\frac{7}{9} \bigcirc -0.77$
29. $\frac{12}{13} \bigcirc 0.9231$
30. $\frac{15}{16} \bigcirc \frac{16}{17}$

31. $-\frac{1}{11} \bigcirc -\frac{1}{13}$
32. $\frac{5}{23} \bigcirc \frac{8}{45}$
33. $4\frac{11}{19} \bigcirc 4.57$

CALCULATOR **Order from least to greatest.**

34. $\frac{3}{8}, \frac{1}{2}, \frac{1}{4}$ _______________________________

35. $-\frac{11}{15}, -\frac{7}{10}, -\frac{3}{5}$ _______________________________

36. $\frac{3}{4}, \frac{7}{12}, \frac{11}{16}$ _______________________________

37. $-\frac{5}{13}, -\frac{7}{15}, -\frac{9}{17}$ _______________________________

38. $3\frac{11}{15}, 3\frac{19}{24}, 3\frac{13}{18}, 3\frac{17}{21}$ _______________________________

Find a rational number between the given rational numbers.

39. $1\frac{1}{2}$ and 2 _________
40. -3 and -4 _________
41. $\frac{5}{7}$ and $\frac{13}{14}$ _________

42. 0 and $\frac{1}{2}$ _________
43. $5\frac{1}{2}$ and 6 _________
44. $\frac{3}{4}$ and $\frac{15}{16}$ _________

■ *Practice*

Adding and Subtracting Rational Numbers

Find each sum or difference.

1. $\frac{2}{3} + \frac{1}{6}$ _______

2. $\frac{5}{8} - \frac{1}{4}$ _______

3. $\frac{9}{16} + \frac{3}{4}$ _______

4. $2 - \frac{5}{7}$ _______

5. $1\frac{1}{2} - 2\frac{4}{5}$ _______

6. $3\frac{5}{6} + 2\frac{3}{4}$ _______

7. $\frac{1}{4} - \frac{1}{3}$ _______

8. $5\frac{7}{8} + 3\frac{5}{12}$ _______

9. $2\frac{7}{10} - 3\frac{7}{20}$ _______

10. $\frac{x}{3} + \frac{x}{5}$ _______

11. $\frac{2n}{5} + \left(-\frac{n}{6}\right)$ _______

12. $1\frac{2}{3}k + 2\frac{1}{4}k$ _______

13. $8\frac{5}{12}p - 9\frac{2}{3}p$ _______

14. $2\frac{11}{15}x + 3\frac{4}{5}x + 4\frac{1}{3}x$ _______

Estimate each sum or difference.

15. $13\frac{4}{5} - 2\frac{9}{10}$ _______

16. $18\frac{3}{8} + 11\frac{6}{7}$ _______

17. $-84\frac{3}{11} + 103\frac{11}{12}$ _______

18. $23\frac{6}{13} + 32\frac{7}{8}$ _______

19. $26\frac{9}{10} + 72\frac{5}{6}$ _______

20. $258\frac{17}{20} - 119\frac{2}{9}$ _______

MENTAL MATH **Find each sum or difference.**

21. $3\frac{3}{8} + 2\frac{1}{8} + 1\frac{3}{8}$ _______

22. $6\frac{7}{12} - 4\frac{5}{12}$ _______

23. $8\frac{3}{16} + 2\frac{5}{16} + 4\frac{7}{16}$ _______

24. $7\frac{9}{10} - 3\frac{3}{10}$ _______

Solve.

25. What fraction of a yard is:

    a. 24 in. _______

    b. 8 in. _______

    c. 1.5 ft _______

    d. 14 in. _______

    e. 42 in. _______

    f. 8 ft _______

    g. 9 in. _______

    h. 11 in. _______

    i. 38 ft _______

26. A picture that is to be framed measures $14\frac{5}{16}$ in. by $9\frac{7}{8}$ in.

    a. How much longer is the picture than it is wide?

    ____

    b. Find the total length of the four pieces that will be used to construct the frame.

    ____

Practice

Working Backwards

Solve each problem by working backwards.

1. Manuel's term paper is due on March 31. He began doing research on March 1. He intends to continue doing research for 3 times as long as he has done already. Then he will spend a week writing the paper and the remaining 3 days typing. What day is it? (Assume he will finish typing on March 30.)

2. A disc jockey must allow time for 24 minutes of commercials every hour, along with 4 minutes for news, 3 minutes for weather, and 2 minutes for public-service announcements. If each record lasts an average of 3 minutes, how many records per hour can the DJ play?

3. Margaret is reading the 713-page novel *War and Peace*. When she has read twice as many pages as she has read already, she will be 119 pages from the end. What page is she on now?

4. On Monday the low temperature at the South Pole dropped 9°F from Sunday's low. On Tuesday it fell another 7°, then rose 13° on Wednesday and 17° more on Thursday. Friday it dropped 8° to −50°F. What was Sunday's low temperature?

5. A guide-dog training center took $\frac{1}{2}$ of the puppies at the dog pound. Steve took $\frac{1}{2}$ of those remaining. Tanya took the 5 that were left. How many puppies were there to begin with?

6. Each problem lists the operations performed on n to produce the given result. Find n.

   a. Multiply by 3, add 4, divide by 5, subtract 6; result, ‑1.

   $n =$ _________

   b. Add 2, divide by 3, subtract 4, multiply by 5; result, 35.

   $n =$ _________

   c. Multiply by 2, add 7, divide by 17; result, 1.

   $n =$ _________

Practice

For use after 5-7 (pp. 206–208)

Multiplying and Dividing Rational Numbers

Find the answer.

1. $\frac{2}{5} \cdot \frac{3}{7}$ _________

2. $\frac{1}{2} \div \frac{5}{8}$ _________

3. $\frac{5}{9} \cdot \frac{3}{5}$ _________

4. $\frac{7}{9} \cdot \frac{6}{13}$ _________

5. $-\frac{5}{24} \div \frac{7}{12}$ _________

6. $\frac{3}{8} \div \frac{6}{7}$ _________

7. $\frac{5}{6} \cdot \left(-1\frac{3}{10}\right)$ _________

8. $\frac{15}{19} \div \frac{15}{19}$ _________

9. $8 \div \frac{4}{5}$ _________

10. $-4\frac{2}{3}\left(-5\frac{1}{6}\right)$ _________

11. $6\frac{1}{4} \div 2\frac{1}{2}$ _________

12. $2\frac{5}{6}\left(-\frac{2}{5}\right)$ _________

13. $5\frac{5}{8} \div 1\frac{1}{4}$ _________

14. $4\frac{7}{8} \cdot 6$ _________

15. $2\frac{1}{3} \div \frac{7}{10}$ _________

Estimate the answer by rounding to the nearest integer.

16. $-4\frac{1}{3} \cdot 3\frac{3}{4}$ _________

17. $8\frac{7}{9} \div 2\frac{5}{6}$ _________

18. $-19\frac{13}{16} \div \left(-4\frac{1}{5}\right)$ _________

19. $8\frac{3}{7} \cdot 8\frac{9}{10}$ _________

20. $-23\frac{3}{4} \div 15\frac{7}{8}$ _________

21. $7.73 \cdot 99\frac{2}{3}$ _________

Compare. Use >, <, or =.

22. $\frac{7}{8} \cdot \frac{4}{5} \bigcirc \frac{7}{8} \div \frac{5}{4}$

23. $\frac{2}{3} \cdot \frac{6}{7} \bigcirc \frac{5}{8} \cdot 1\frac{1}{7}$

24. $-2\frac{1}{3} \cdot 4\frac{1}{8} \bigcirc 36 \div \left(-3\frac{3}{5}\right)$

25. $29\frac{1}{4} \div 4\frac{7}{8} \bigcirc 4\frac{3}{4} \cdot 1\frac{1}{3}$

26. $1\frac{7}{8} \div 1\frac{7}{8} \bigcirc 9 \cdot \frac{1}{9}$

27. $\frac{1}{2} \cdot \frac{2}{3} \cdot \frac{3}{4} \bigcirc \frac{1}{3} \cdot \frac{3}{4} \cdot \frac{4}{5}$

Write each answer in simplest form.

28. $\frac{1}{2} \cdot \frac{6}{9} \cdot \frac{7}{11} \cdot \frac{1}{7}$ _________________________

29. $\frac{3}{5} \cdot \frac{4}{7} \cdot \frac{8}{9} \cdot \frac{15}{32}$ _________________________

30. $\frac{1}{2} \cdot 1\frac{7}{8} \cdot \frac{1}{5} \cdot \frac{9}{12}$ _________________________

31. $\frac{4}{9} \cdot \frac{3}{7} \cdot \frac{2}{5} \cdot 1\frac{11}{24}$ _________________________

32. $3\frac{1}{4} \cdot 1\frac{3}{5} \cdot 2\frac{5}{8}$ _________________________

33. $2\frac{1}{3} \cdot 2\frac{5}{8} \cdot 2\frac{2}{7}$ _________________________

34. $11 \div 3\frac{1}{7} \div \left(2\frac{3}{4} - \frac{1}{12}\right)$ _________________________

35. $8 \div 2\frac{3}{4} \div \left(\frac{4}{9} - \frac{4}{5}\right)$ _________________________

Chapter 5

▬ *Practice*

Rational Numbers with Exponents

Evaluate.

1. 1^{-3} _________

2. $(-3)^{-3}$ _________

3. 5^{-2} _________

4. 9^{-2} _________

5. 3^{-2} _________

6. $(-5)^{-2}$ _________

7. 2^{-5} _________

8. 8^0 _________

9. $(-4)^{-3}$ _________

10. $\dfrac{3^4}{3^7}$ _________

11. 12^{-1} _________

12. $(-1)^{-5}$ _________

13. $\dfrac{9^9}{9^4}$ _________

14. $\dfrac{5^1}{5^5}$ _________

15. $\dfrac{11^8}{11^{13}}$ _________

16. $\dfrac{7^0}{7^1}$ _________

Write with positive or negative exponents. Leave no exponents in the denominator.

17. $\dfrac{a^3}{a^7}$ _________

18. $\dfrac{l^5}{l^6}$ _________

19. $\dfrac{d^3}{d^{-10}}$ _________

20. $\dfrac{x^7}{x^7}$ _________

21. $\dfrac{k^5}{k^9}$ _________

22. $\dfrac{3y^4}{6y^{-4}}$ _________

23. $\dfrac{9x^8}{12x^5}$ _________

24. $\dfrac{2f^{10}}{f^5}$ _________

25. $\dfrac{3xy^4}{9xy^{-4}}$ _________

26. $\dfrac{4x^2y}{2x^3}$ _________

27. $\dfrac{n^{-4}}{n^{-6}}$ _________

28. $\dfrac{15h^6k^{-3}}{5hk^{-2}}$ _________

29. $\dfrac{15mn^{-5}}{12m^{-3}n^{-5}}$ _________

30. $\dfrac{32a^3b^{-4}c}{36a^{-7}b^2d^5}$ _________

Write with positive exponents.

31. $\dfrac{24x^6}{6x}$ _________

32. $\dfrac{7k^3}{k^5}$ _________

33. $\dfrac{6m^{-2}n^4}{8m^{-1}n^5}$ _________

34. $\dfrac{a^5b^{-4}}{a^{-4}b^5}$ _________

35. $\dfrac{10c^5d^4}{15cd^4}$ _________

36. $\dfrac{x^0y^{-1}z^2}{x^{-5}y^{-4}z^{-3}}$ _________

Write each of these numbers without an exponent.

37. -2^4 _________

38. $(-2)^0$ _________

39. 2^{-4} _________

40. $(-2)^{-4}$ _________

41. -2^0 _________

42. $(-2)^4$ _________

43. 2^0 _________

44. $(-2)^{-1}$ _________

Simplify.

45. $(2x)^3$ _________

46. $(-3y^2)^2$ _________

47. $(5ab^{-2})^3$ _________

48. $(12mn)^2$ _________

49. $(-10xy^3)^3$ _________

50. $(9qrs^{-4})^3$ _________

51. $k^{-3} \cdot k^5 \cdot k^{-2}$ _________

52. $\left(\dfrac{2x^{-1}}{y}\right)^2 \left(\dfrac{3y^{-2}}{x}\right)^3$ _________

Practice

Addition and Subtraction Equations

Solve each equation.

1. $x + \frac{5}{8} = \frac{7}{8}$ _______

2. $k + \frac{4}{5} = 1\frac{3}{5}$ _______

3. $4 = \frac{4}{9} + y$ _______

4. $h + \left(-\frac{5}{8}\right) = -\frac{5}{12}$ _______

5. $n + \frac{2}{3} = \frac{1}{9}$ _______

6. $e - \frac{11}{16} = -\frac{7}{8}$ _______

7. $m - \left(-\frac{7}{10}\right) = -1\frac{1}{5}$ _______

8. $k - \frac{3}{4} = \frac{2}{5}$ _______

9. $x - \frac{5}{6} = \frac{1}{10}$ _______

10. $t - \left(-3\frac{1}{6}\right) = 7\frac{2}{3}$ _______

11. $w - 14\frac{1}{12} = -2\frac{3}{4}$ _______

12. $v + \left(-4\frac{5}{6}\right) = 2\frac{1}{3}$ _______

13. $a - 9\frac{1}{6} = -3\frac{19}{24}$ _______

14. $f + \left|-3\frac{11}{12}\right| = 18$ _______

15. $z + (-3.4) = |-4.1|$ _______

16. $x - \frac{7}{15} = \frac{7}{60}$ _______

17. $h - \left(-6\frac{1}{2}\right) = 14\frac{1}{4}$ _______

18. $p - 5\frac{3}{8} = -\frac{11}{24}$ _______

MENTAL MATH Solve each equation.

19. $x + \frac{3}{7} = \frac{5}{7}$ _______

20. $k - \frac{8}{9} = -\frac{1}{9}$ _______

21. $a + \frac{1}{9} = \frac{3}{9}$ _______

22. $g - \frac{4}{5} = -\frac{2}{5}$ _______

23. $h + \frac{3}{4} = \frac{7}{8}$ _______

24. $e + 1\frac{13}{16} = 2\frac{5}{16}$ _______

25. $m + \frac{5}{8} = -\frac{3}{16}$ _______

26. $p - 4\frac{5}{12} = 2\frac{7}{12}$ _______

Write an equation and solve.

27. On Tuesday, the price of a share of XYZ stock fell $5\frac{3}{4}$ from Monday's closing price, to $18\frac{7}{8}$. What was Monday's closing price?

____

28. Pete's papaya tree grew $3\frac{7}{12}$ ft during the year. If its height at the end of the year was $21\frac{1}{6}$ ft, what was its height at the beginning of the year?

____

29. Lynn is $1\frac{3}{4}$ ft taller than Jay. If Jay is $4\frac{1}{2}$ ft tall, how tall is Lynn?

____

Practice

Multiplication Equations

Solve each equation.

1. $\frac{3}{4}x = \frac{9}{16}$ _______

2. $-\frac{1}{3}p = \frac{1}{4}$ _______

3. $\frac{4}{7}y = 4$ _______

4. $\frac{-3}{8}k = \frac{1}{2}$ _______

5. $\frac{1}{8}h = \frac{1}{10}$ _______

6. $\frac{10}{11}n = \frac{2}{11}$ _______

7. $2\frac{2}{3}e = \frac{3}{4}$ _______

8. $-1\frac{2}{7}m = 6$ _______

9. $2\frac{1}{4}f = \frac{6}{5}$ _______

10. $-\frac{1}{4}p = \frac{1}{18}$ _______

11. $\frac{11}{-12}w = -1$ _______

12. $\frac{7}{8}c = \frac{7}{6}$ _______

13. $-3\frac{4}{7}x = 0$ _______

14. $\frac{2}{3}m = 2\frac{2}{9}$ _______

15. $\frac{1}{5}k = -\frac{1}{3}$ _______

For what values of x, if any, is each equation true?

16. $|x| = \frac{5}{8}$ _______

17. $|x| = -\frac{2}{3}$ _______

18. $\frac{1}{2}|x| = \frac{3}{4}$ _______

19. $\frac{-4}{5}|x| = -\frac{1}{3}$ _______

20. $4\frac{1}{2}|x| = 5\frac{5}{8}$ _______

21. $-1\frac{2}{3}|x| = 4\frac{1}{6}$ _______

Write an equation and solve each problem.

22. There are 3 outs in a baseball inning. Belinsky got 22 outs before he was replaced by a relief pitcher. How many innings did he pitch? Let p represent the number of innings.

____

23. Floor boards are $8\frac{3}{8}$ in. wide. How many must be laid side by side to cover a floor 201 in. wide? Let n represent the number .

____

24. It takes Nancy $1\frac{2}{3}$ min to read 1 page in her social studies book. It took her $22\frac{1}{2}$ min to complete her reading assignment. How long was the assignment? Let m represent the number of pages she read.

____

25. It takes Gary three hours to drive to Boston. If the trip is 156 miles, what is Gary's average number of miles per hour? Let x represent the miles per hour.

____

Practice

Ratios, Proportions, and Rates

Write each ratio as a fraction in lowest terms.

1. 7:12 _________
2. 3 is to 6 _________
3. 9 out of 21 _________
4. 10:45 _________
5. 32 out of 40 _________
6. 24 is to 18 _________
7. 36 is to 60 _________
8. 13 out of 14 _________
9. 45:63 _________

Write three ratios each to describe the figures.

10. _________

11. _________

12. _________

Write each ratio as a fraction in lowest terms.

	Boys	Girls
8th Grade	26	34
9th Grade	30	22

13. 8th-grade boys to 9th-grade boys _________
14. 8th-grade girls to 8th-grade boys _________
15. 8th graders to 9th graders _________
16. boys to girls _________
17. girls to all students _________

Compare. Write = or ≠.

18. $\frac{3}{4}$ ☐ $\frac{9}{12}$
19. $\frac{25}{40}$ ☐ $\frac{5}{8}$
20. $\frac{15}{20}$ ☐ $\frac{12}{15}$

21. $\frac{8}{12}$ ☐ $\frac{14}{21}$
22. $\frac{13}{15}$ ☐ $\frac{4}{5}$
23. $\frac{42}{35}$ ☐ $\frac{36}{30}$

24. $\frac{4}{5}$ ☐ $\frac{5}{6}$
25. $\frac{49}{21}$ ☐ $\frac{28}{12}$
26. $\frac{64}{72}$ ☐ $\frac{72}{81}$

27. Of Exercises 18–26, which pairs of ratios form proportions?
Write the numbers of the exercises.

____

CALCULATOR Compare. Write = or ≠.

28. $\frac{138}{161}$ ☐ $\frac{246}{287}$
29. $\frac{136}{221}$ ☐ $\frac{159}{265}$
30. $\frac{356}{801}$ ☐ $\frac{292}{657}$

Express as a unit rate.

31. 78 mi on 3 gal _________
32. $52.50 in 7 h _________
33. 416 mi in 8 h _________
34. 9 bull's eyes in 117 throws _________

____

Practice

Solving Proportions

Solve.

1. $\frac{3}{5} = \frac{15}{x}$ _______

2. $\frac{15}{30} = \frac{n}{34}$ _______

3. $\frac{6}{p} = \frac{18}{42}$ _______

4. $\frac{h}{36} = \frac{21}{27}$ _______

5. $\frac{11}{6} = \frac{f}{60}$ _______

6. $\frac{y}{9} = \frac{26}{6}$ _______

7. $\frac{26}{15} = \frac{130}{m}$ _______

8. $\frac{36}{j} = \frac{15}{20}$ _______

9. $\frac{63}{t} = \frac{14}{16}$ _______

10. $\frac{r}{23} = \frac{17}{34}$ _______

11. $\frac{77.5}{93} = \frac{x}{24}$ _______

12. $\frac{7}{20} = \frac{e}{70}$ _______

Each pair of figures is in proportion. Find the missing lengths.

13. 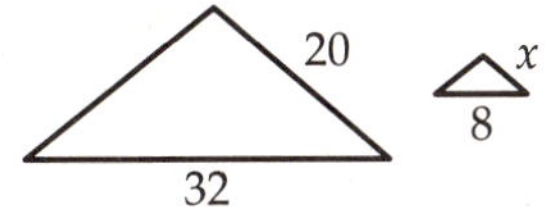

$x = $ _______

14. 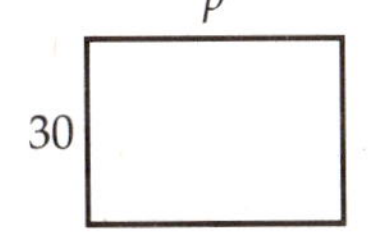

$p = $ _______

15. 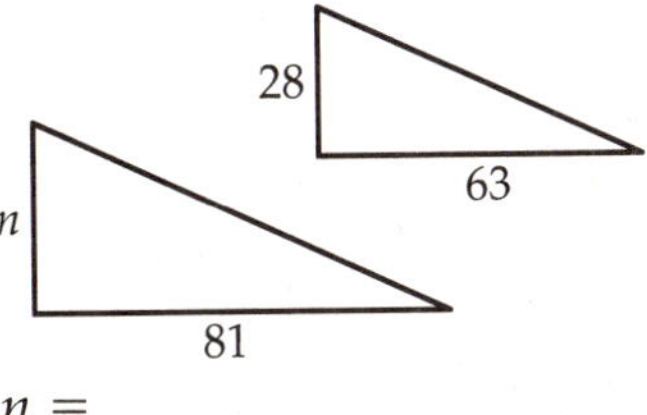

$n = $ _______

16. 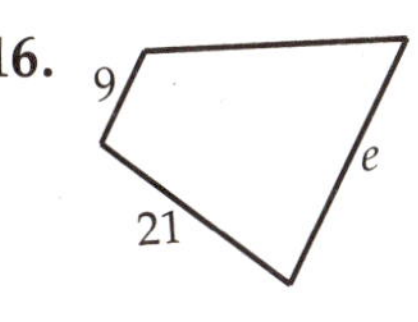

$e = $ _______ $f = $ _______

Write a proportion to describe each situation. Then solve.

17. 420 ft^2 painted in 36 min; f ft^2 painted in 30 min

____

18. 75 points scored in 6 games; p points scored in 4 games

____

19. 6 apples for \$1.00; 15 apples for d dollars

____

Solve.

20. If $\frac{x}{9} = \frac{7}{12}$, find the ratio of x to 7. _______

21. If $\frac{12}{15} = \frac{y}{25}$, find the ratio of y to 12. _______

22. If $\frac{8}{3} = \frac{40}{k}$, find the ratio of k to 3. _______

Practice

Percent

Write each ratio as a percent.

1. 9:12 _______________
2. 16:20 _______________
3. 17:34 _______________
4. 49:70 _______________
5. 19:76 _______________
6. 81:90 _______________
7. 21:35 _______________
8. 21:56 _______________
9. 39:60 _______________
10. 27:75 _______________
11. 42:48 _______________
12. 65:52 _______________

Write each decimal as a percent.

13. 0.16 _______________
14. 0.72 _______________
15. 0.08 _______________
16. 0.99 _______________
17. 0.4 _______________
18. 1 _______________
19. 0.036 _______________
20. 0.777 _______________
21. 3.04 _______________
22. 0.002 _______________
23. 0.0004 _______________
24. 5.009 _______________

Write each fraction as a percent.

25. $\frac{7}{10}$ _______________
26. $\frac{3}{5}$ _______________
27. $\frac{11}{20}$ _______________
28. $\frac{17}{25}$ _______________
29. $\frac{1}{5}$ _______________
30. $\frac{39}{100}$ _______________
31. $\frac{1}{20}$ _______________
32. $\frac{13}{50}$ _______________
33. $\frac{24}{25}$ _______________
34. $\frac{31}{40}$ _______________
35. $\frac{111}{200}$ _______________
36. $\frac{403}{1,000}$ _______________

CALCULATOR Write each fraction as a percent. Round to the nearest tenth of a percent.

37. $\frac{4}{7}$ _______________
38. $\frac{57}{99}$ _______________
39. $\frac{40}{13}$ _______________

Compare. Use <, >, or =.

40. $\frac{1}{3}$ ☐ 33%   41. $\frac{3}{100}$ ☐ 3%   42. 55% ☐ 55   43. 0.7 ☐ 7%   44. 80% ☐ $\frac{4}{5}$

Practice

Using Proportions to Find Percent

Write and solve a proportion for each.

1. What percent of 40 is 12? _________
2. What percent of 75 is 60? _________
3. What percent of 48 is 18? _________
4. What percent is 17 of 25? _________
5. What percent is 54 of 60? _________
6. What percent of 68 is 51? _________
7. What percent is 39 of 50? _________
8. What percent of 52 is 65? _________
9. Find 80% of 25. _________
10. Find 75% of 76. _________
11. Find 150% of 74. _________
12. Find $27\frac{1}{2}$% of 96. _________
13. Find 44% of 375. _________
14. Find 24% of 120. _________
15. Find 65% of 180. _________
16. Find 260% of 30. _________
17. 40% of x is 28. What is x? _________
18. 75% of p is 12. What is p? _________
19. 9% of k is 27. What is k? _________
20. $62\frac{1}{2}$% of t is 35. What is t? _________
21. 38% of n is 33.44. What is n? _________
22. 120% of y is 42. What is y? _________
23. 300% of m is 600. What is m? _________
24. 1.5% of h is 12. What is h? _________

Solve.

25. The Eagles won 70% of the 40 games that they played. How many games did they win?

____

26. Thirty-five of 40 students surveyed said that they favored recycling. What percent of those surveyed favored recycling?

____

27. Candidate Carson received 2,310 votes, 55% of the total. How many total votes were cast?

____

Practice

Percents and Equations

Write and solve an equation to find each. Use a triangle diagram if necessary.

1. What percent of 25 is 17? _________
2. What percent of 40 is 26? _________
3. What percent is 10 of 8? _________
4. What percent of 32 is 28? _________
5. What percent is 63 of 84? _________
6. What percent is 84 of 60? _________
7. What percent is 3 of 600? _________
8. What percent is 22 of 4? _________
9. Find 45% of 60. _________
10. Find 37.5% of 104. _________
11. Find 325% of 52. _________
12. Find 68% of 150. _________
13. Find $66\frac{2}{3}$% of 87. _________
14. Find 0.4% of 25. _________
15. Find 1% of 3,620. _________
16. Find 180% of 65. _________
17. $62\frac{1}{2}$% of x is 5. What is x? _________________
18. 300% of k is 42. What is k? _________________
19. $33\frac{1}{3}$% of p is 19. What is p? _________________
20. 70% of c is 49. What is c? _________________
21. 15% of n is 1,050. What is n? _________________
22. 38% of y is 494. What is y? _________________
23. $183\frac{1}{3}$% of m is 209. What is m? _________________
24. 0.4% of h is 276. What is h? _________________

Solve.

25. How much interest will be earned in one year on a deposit of $1,400 invested at $6\frac{1}{2}$% simple interest?

____

26. A camera regularly priced at $295 was placed on sale at $236. What percent of the regular price was the sale price?

____

27. 936 students, 65% of the entire student body, attended the football game. Find the size of the student body.

____

Practice

Percent of Change

Find each percent of increase.

1. 40 is increased to 45. ________________
2. 33 is increased to 55. ________________
3. 15 is increased to 34. ________________
4. 11 is increased to 88. ________________
5. 72 is increased to 117. ________________
6. 28 is increased to 49. ________________
7. 35 is increased to 49. ________________
8. 48 is increased to 132. ________________

Find each percent of decrease.

9. 60 is decreased to 15. ________________
10. 56 is decreased to 35. ________________
11. 140 is decreased to 77. ________________
12. 96 is decreased to 64. ________________
13. 99 is decreased to 69. ________________
14. 50 is decreased to 44. ________________
15. 83 is decreased to 0. ________________
16. 475 is decreased to 152. ________________

Find each percent of change. Label your answer as increase (I) or decrease (D).

17. 24 to 21 ________________
18. 64 to 80 ________________
19. 100 to 113 ________________
20. 50 to 41 ________________
21. 63 to 105 ________________
22. 42 to 168 ________________
23. 80 to 24 ________________
24. 200 to 158 ________________

MENTAL MATH **Find each percent of change. Label your answer as increase (I) or decrease (D).**

25. 20 to 24 ________________
26. 44 to 22 ________________
27. 16 to 12 ________________
28. 10 to 100 ________________
29. 20 to 40 ________________
30. 10 to 50 ________________
31. 12 to 16 ________________
32. 80 to 100 ________________

CALCULATOR **Find each percent of change. Round your answer to the nearest hundredth. Label your answer as increase (I) or decrease (D).**

33. 56 to 71 ________________
34. 127 to 84 ________________
35. 63.7 to 42.9 ________________
36. 119 to 306.4 ________________
37. 69 to 117 ________________
38. 19 to 9 ________________
39. 95 to 145 ________________
40. 88 to 26 ________________

Practice

Draw a Diagram

Solve using a diagram.

1. A hot-air balloon drifted 13 mi south, 8 mi east, 17 mi north, 15 mi west, and 4 mi south. How far was the balloon from its starting point?

2. Four students are standing in line. Art is behind Doug. Brenda is ahead of Connie. Doug is behind Connie. Find the order of the four.

3. Tom weighs 20% more than Fred, 10% less than Pete, and 20% less than Mike. Fred weighs 120 lb. Find the weights of Tom, Pete, and Mike.

4. The diagram shows that 2 diagonals can be drawn from a given vertex (corner) in a 5-sided figure. 

   a. How many diagonals can be drawn from a given vertex of a 6-sided figure; a 7-sided figure?

   b. Predict the number of diagonals that can be drawn from a given vertex of a 147-sided figure.

5. Two cars started at the same point and traveled in opposite directions. One went 50 mi/h, the other 60 mi/h. After 1 h, the faster car turned around and started chasing the slower. Two hours later, how far apart were the cars and which one was in the lead?

6. The Hawaiian volcano Mauna Kea is 33,476 ft high, with 19,680 ft of its height below the ocean. The top of a lighthouse standing at sea level is 13,711 ft below the top of Mauna Kea. A shark is swimming 19,277 ft above the base of the volcano. Find the difference in elevation from the shark to the top of the lighthouse.

Practice

Two-step Equations

Solve each equation.

1. $4x - 17 = 31$ __________

2. $15 = 2m + 3$ __________

3. $\frac{k}{3} + 3 = 8$ __________

4. $7 = 3 + \frac{h}{6}$ __________

5. $9n + 18 = 81$ __________

6. $5 = \frac{y}{3} - 9$ __________

7. $14 = 5k - 31$ __________

8. $\frac{t}{9} - 7 = -5$ __________

9. $\frac{v}{8} - 9 = -13$ __________

10. $25 - 13f = -14$ __________

11. $18p - 45 = 0$ __________

12. $\frac{2}{3}y - 6 = 2$ __________

13. $40 - 5n = -2$ __________

14. $\frac{7}{8}h - \frac{5}{8} = 2$ __________

MENTAL MATH **Solve each equation.**

15. $3p + 5 = 14$ __________

16. $\frac{k}{2} - 5 = 1$ __________

17. $\frac{m}{7} - 3 = 0$ __________

18. $10v - 6 = 24$ __________

CALCULATOR **Solve each equation.**

19. $9w - 16.3 = 5.3$ __________

20. $88.1 - 2.3f = 72.46$ __________

21. $-15.3 = -7.5k + 55.2$ __________

22. $26e + 891 = -71$ __________

Choose the correct equation. Solve.

23. Tehira has read 110 pages of a 290-page book. She reads 20 pages each day. How many days will it take to finish?

    a. $20 + 110p = 290$

    b. $20p + 290 = 110$

    c. $110 + 20p = 290$

    d. $290 = 110 - 20p$

Write an equation to describe the situation. Solve.

24. A waitress earned \$73 for 6 hours of work. The total included \$46 in tips. What was her hourly wage?

25. A car rented for \$29 per day plus \$0.08 per mile. Julia paid \$46.12 for a one-day rental. How far did she drive?

Practice

Simplifying and Solving Equations

Solve and check each equation.

1. $\frac{p}{3} - 7 = -2$ _____________
2. $2(n - 7) + 3 = 9$ _____________
3. $0 = 5(k + 9)$ _____________
4. $4h + 7h - 16 = 6$ _____________
5. $3(2n - 7) = 9$ _____________
6. $-27 = 8x - 5x$ _____________
7. $4p + 5 - 7p = -1$ _____________
8. $7 - y + 5y = 9$ _____________
9. $8e + 3(5 - e) = 10$ _____________
10. $h + 3h + 4h = 100$ _____________
11. $1.2m + 7.5m + 2.1 = 63$ _____________
12. $14 = \frac{2}{3}(9y - 15)$ _____________
13. $-37 = 3x + 11 - 7x$ _____________
14. $9 - 3(n - 5) = 30$ _____________
15. $\frac{1}{6}(y + 42) - 15 = -3$ _____________
16. $0.7n - 1.5 + 7.3n = 14.5$ _____________

MENTAL MATH Find each value.

17. If $2(x + 7) = 24$, find the value of $2x$. _____________
18. If $y + 4y + 8y = 19$, find the value of $13y$. _____________
19. If $\frac{1}{3}(5k + 2) = 7$, find the value of $5k + 2$. _____________
20. If $7n + 3n = 46$, find the value of n. _____________

CALCULATOR Solve each equation.

21. $16.3k + 19.2 + 7.5k = -64.1$ _____________
22. $93.96 = 4.7p + 8.7p - 2.6p$ _____________
23. $2.3(x + 1.4) = -9.66$ _____________
24. $\frac{1}{8.3}(x - 17.7) + 19.6 = 27.8$ _____________

Write an equation to describe the situation. Solve.

25. Jolene bought three blouses at one price and 2 blouses priced $3 below the others. The total cost was $91.50. Find the prices of the blouses.

____

26. Jack's overtime wage is $3 per hour more than his regular hourly wage. He worked for 5 hours at his regular wage and 4 hours at the overtime wage. He earned $66. Find his regular wage.

____

Practice

Writing Equations

Write an equation. Do not solve.

1. The sum of half of a number and 8 less than the number is 25.

2. The product of 6 and 3 more than k is 48.

Write an equation. Solve.

3. Bill purchased 4 pens for $3.32, including $.16 sales tax. Find the cost of 1 pen.

4. Arnold had $1.70 in dimes and quarters. He had 3 more dimes than quarters. How many of each coin did he have?

5. A baby weighed 3.2 kg at birth. She gained 0.17 kg per week. How old was she when she weighed 5.75 kg?

6. In the parking lot at a truck stop there were 6 more cars than 18-wheel trucks. There were 134 wheels in the parking lot. How many cars and trucks were there?

7. A bottle and a cap together cost $1.10. The bottle cost $1 more than the cap. How much did each cost?

8. Orlando worked for $6/h one week and $7/h the next week. He worked 5 more hours the second week than the first and earned $347 for the 2 weeks of work. How many hours did he work each week?

9. A triangle has two sides equal in length and a third side 5 in. longer than half the length of each of the other two sides. If the perimeter of the triangle is 50 in., how long is each side?

Practice

Equations with Variables on Both Sides

MENTAL MATH Solve.

1. $n + n + n + n = n + n + n + 10$ _________

2. $5x + 7 = 6x$ _________   3. $k + 12 = 3k$ _________

4. $8m = 5m + 12$ _________   5. $3p - 9 = 4p$ _________

Solve each equation.

6. $3k + 16 = 5k$ _________   7. $5e = 3e + 36$ _________

8. $n + 4n - 22 = 7n$ _________   9. $2(x - 7) = 3x$ _________

10. $8h - 10h = 3h + 25$ _________   11. $7n + 6n - 5 = 4n + 4$ _________

12. $11(p - 3) = 5(p + 3)$ _________   13. $9(m + 2) = -6(m + 7)$ _________

14. $y + 2(y - 5) = 2y + 2$ _________   15. $-9x + 7 = 3x + 19$ _________

16. $0.2n + 13 = 1.3n - 14.5$ _________   17. $-6(4 - t) = 12t$ _________

18. $\frac{1}{2}(e - 6) = \frac{1}{4}(e + 6)$ _________   19. $5m + 9 = 3(m - 5) + 7$ _________

20. $\frac{2}{3}p + 12 = \frac{3}{5}p + 10$ _________   21. $x + 7x + 15x = 29x + 18$ _________

22. $3(x + 7) + 2(x - 5) = x - 5$ _________   23. $5g = 6g$ _________

Is the given number a solution of the equation?

24. $k + 9 = 6(k - 11)$, $k = 15$ _________

25. $2(x + 7) = 5(x - 7)$, $x = 3$ _________

26. $8(7 - p) - 8 = -16(p - 2)$, $p = -2$ _________

CALCULATOR Solve.

27. $3.2c + 9.4 - 0.8c = 3(c - 2.4) + 7.6$ _________

28. $6.9(3.5x - 2.7) = 2.3(2.1x + 17.1)$ _________

Write an equation. Solve.

29. The difference when 7 less than a number is subtracted from twice the number is 12. What is the number?

____

30. Four less than three times a number is three more than two times the number. What is the number?

____

Practice

Inequalities and Their Graphs

Tell whether each inequality is true or false. Write *T* or *F*.

1. $-8 > 5 - 13$ _________

2. $0 \leq -4 + 6$ _________

3. $|9 - 17| \geq 8$ _________

4. $2(7 - 9) > 3(-6) + 15$ _________

5. $\frac{2}{3}(10 - 25) \leq (-2)^3$ _________

CALCULATOR Write *T* or *F*.

6. $|7.65 - 11.03| \leq 3.5(5.74 - 4.83)$ _________

7. $-4.65(-2.91) > 3.86(5.71 - 2.36)$ _________

8. $(2.7 - 5.3)(6.4 - 11.9) \leq 0.4|14.91 - 50.66|$ _________

Write each inequality as a word sentence.

9. $17 < k$

____

10. $x \leq 2.9$

____

11. $|p| \geq 13$

____

State an inequality for each graph.

12. _________

13. _________

14. _________

15. _________

Graph each inequality on the number line.

16. $m \leq 5$

17. $k > 0$

18. $y < -2$

19. $c \geq -4$

Write an inequality for each word phrase.

20. A number n is negative. _________________

21. The sum of x and y is less than or equal to -2. _________________

22. A number h is not less than 7. _________________

Practice

Solving One-step Inequalities

Answer _true_ or _false_.

1. When a negative number is added to both sides of an inequality, the inequality is reversed.

   ____

2. When both sides of an inequality are multiplied by a negative number, the inequality is reversed.

   ____

What was done to both sides of the first inequality to obtain the second?

3. $p - 7 > 14$; $p > 21$ _______________________

4. $4 \leq -4y$; $-1 \geq y$ _______________________

5. $\frac{1}{8}n < -2$; $n < -16$ _______________________

Tell whether each number is a solution of $7 \geq 3k - 2$.

6. 4 _________   7. -2 _________   8. 0 _________   9. 3 _________

Solve each inequality for the variable x.

10. $7 + x \geq 9$ _________   11. $-5x < 10$ _________   12. $\frac{x}{4} > 1$ _________

13. $-5 \leq x - 6$ _________   14. $-8 < -8x$ _________   15. $\frac{1}{3}x > -2$ _________

16. $0 \geq x + 12$ _________   17. $x - 15 \leq -8$ _________   18. $\frac{2}{3}x < -6$ _________

19. $-2.6 < \frac{x}{-10}$ _________   20. $13 + x \geq 13$ _________   21. $-x \leq 2$ _________

Write an inequality for each word phrase. Solve.

22. Six less than n is less than -4. Find n. ____

23. The product of k and -5 is no more than 30. Find k. _______________________________________

24. Half of p is at least -7. Find p. ____

25. Six more than 3 times n is greater than -7. Find n. _______________________________

26. The product of k and 9 is no more than 15. Find k. _______________________________

27. One-third of p is at least -17. Find p. _______________________________________

28. The opposite of g is at least -5. Find g. _______________________________________

Practice

Solving Two-step Inequalities

What was done to each side of the first inequality to obtain the second?

1. $4 - 7x \le 2$; $-7x \le -2$ ___________________________

2. $\frac{x}{-3} > 1$; $x < -3$ ___________________________

3. $5x - 6 \ge 2$; $5x \ge 8$ ___________________________

4. $-6x < 12$; $x > -2$ ___________________________

Solve for x.

5. $2x - 5 > 1$ __________

6. $5x + 2 \le 17$ __________

7. $3 < \frac{1}{2}x + 1$ __________

8. $7x + 2x \ge 21 - 3$ __________

9. $-8x + 18 > -22$ __________

10. $9 - x > 10$ __________

11. $\frac{1}{5}x + 6 > -3$ __________

12. $19 + 8 \le 6 + 7x$ __________

13. $\frac{x}{-4} > 0$ __________

14. $9x - 7 \le 38$ __________

15. $3x + 11x \le -42$ __________

16. $-12 < -12x$ __________

17. $\frac{1}{7}x + 5 > 0$ __________

18. $50 < 8 - 6x$ __________

19. $3(x - 9) > -18$ __________

20. $30 \ge -6(5 - x)$ __________

Write an inequality that describes each situation. Then solve.

21. Nine more than half the number n is no more than -8. Find n.

____

22. Judith drove h hours at a rate of 55 mi/hr. She did not reach her goal of driving 385 miles for the day. How long did she drive?

____

23. The average age of the four Berger children is at least 15. The ages of three of the children are 19, 14, and 12. What is the age of the fourth child?

____

24. Five less than three times the number k is neither less than nor equal to 19. Find k.

____

Practice

The Coordinate Plane

Write the letter of the point named by each ordered pair.

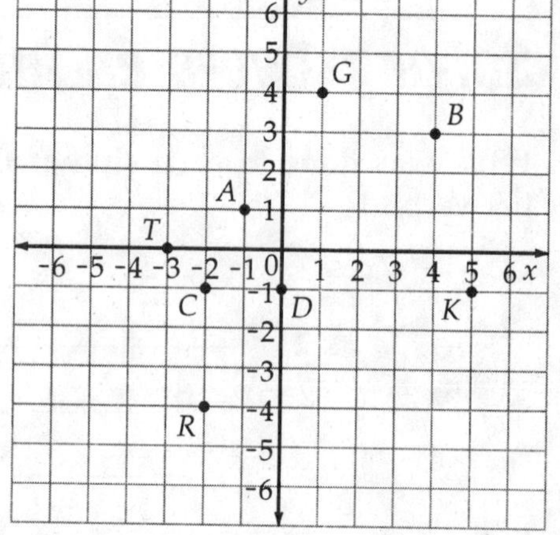

1. $(1, 4)$ __________   2. $(-3, 0)$ __________

3. $(5, -1)$ __________   4. $(-2, -4)$ __________

Write the coordinates of each point.

5. A __________   6. B __________

7. C __________   8. D __________

Graph each point. Write the letter beside the point.

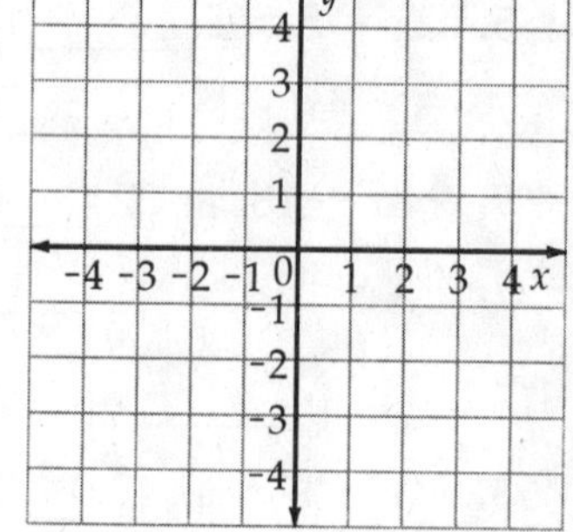

9. $A(-2, 2)$ 10. $B(0, 3)$ 11. $C(2, -2)$

12. $D(-3, 0)$ 13. $E(2, 3)$ 14. $F(0, 0)$

15. $G(-1, -2)$ 16. $H\left(1\frac{1}{2}, -1\frac{1}{2}\right)$

Complete using positive or negative. Write p or n.

17. In Quadrant II, x is __________ and y is __________ .

18. In Quadrant III, x is __________ and y is __________ .

19. Point P is below the x-axis and right of the y-axis. The x-coordinate of P is ▮ and the y-coordinate is ▮.

____

In which quadrant or on what axis does each point fall?

20. $(3, -5)$ __________   21. $(|-7|, |-23|)$ __________   22. $(0, 35.7)$ __________   23. $(-83, 0)$ __________

24. $P(-2, 3)$, $Q(5, 3)$, and $R(-2, -6)$ are three vertices of a rectangle. Find the coordinates of the fourth vertex.

____

25. A circle with center at the origin passes through the points $A(-7, 0)$, $B(7, 0)$, and $C(0, y)$. Find the two possible values of y.

____

26. The point $G(x, y)$ is directly above $E(-2, 7)$ and directly to the right of $F(-4, 12)$. Find x and y.

____

Practice

For use after 8-2 (pp. 320–323)

Solving Equations

MENTAL MATH Is each ordered pair a solution of $3x - 2y = 12$?
Write *yes* or *no*.

1. $(0, 4)$ ________

2. $(6, 3)$ ________

3. $(4, 0)$ ________

Is each ordered pair a solution of $3x - 2y = 12$?

4. $(-3, 2)$ ________

5. $(10, 9)$ ________

6. $(-16, -30)$ ________

7. $(8.4, 6.6)$ ________

8. $(-12.6, -24.9)$ ________

9. $(-3.5, -11.25)$ ________

Find the value of y that corresponds to each value of x.

10. $4x + 2y = 2$ if $x = -1$

$y = $ ________

11. $\frac{2}{3}x - y = 11$ if $x = 9$

$y = $ ________

12. $3x + y - 12 = 0$ if $x = 3.5$

$y = $ ________

13. $-2y + 21 = 7x$ if $x = 5$

$y = $ ________

14. $-\frac{1}{2}x + 5y = 47$ if $x = -14$

$y = $ ________

15. $1.8x + 2.6y = 11.6$ if $x = 18$

$y = $ ________

Solve for y in terms of x.

16. $3y = 15x - 12$

$y = $ ________

17. $5x + 10 = 10y$

$y = $ ________

18. $3y - 21 = 12x$

$y = $ ________

19. $5y + 3 = 2y - 3x + 5$

$y = $ ________

20. $-2(x + 3y) = 18$

$y = $ ________

21. $5(x + y) = 20 + 3x$

$y = $ ________

Solve for y in terms of x. Find three solutions of each equation.

22. $x + \frac{1}{3}y = 2$

$y = $ ________

_________ , _________ , _________

23. $8x + 5 = 2y + 1$

$y = $ ________

_________ , _________ , _________

24. $6y - 3x + 18 = 0$

$y = $ ________

_________ , _________ , _________

25. $7\frac{1}{2}x + 1\frac{1}{2}y = 15$

$y = $ ________

_________ , _________ , _________

Practice

Graphing Linear Equations

Find the x-intercept and y-intercept for each equation.

1. $3x + 3y = 9$ _______________

2. $-4y = 16x - 8$ _______________

3. $\frac{3}{4}x = y$ _______________

4. $-2(x - y) = 10$ _______________

Graph.

5. $x + y = 3$

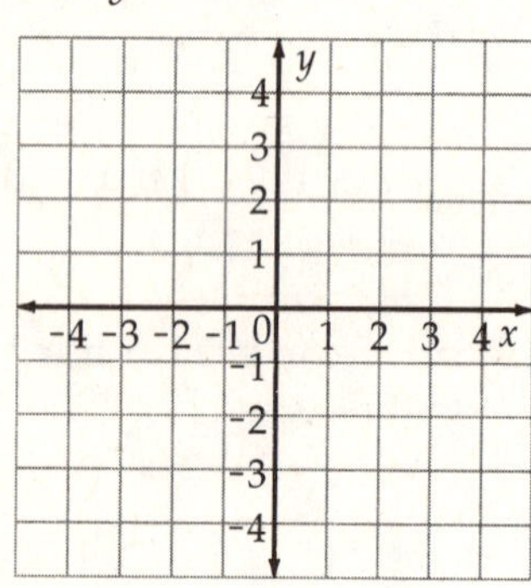

6. $y = 2x - 1$

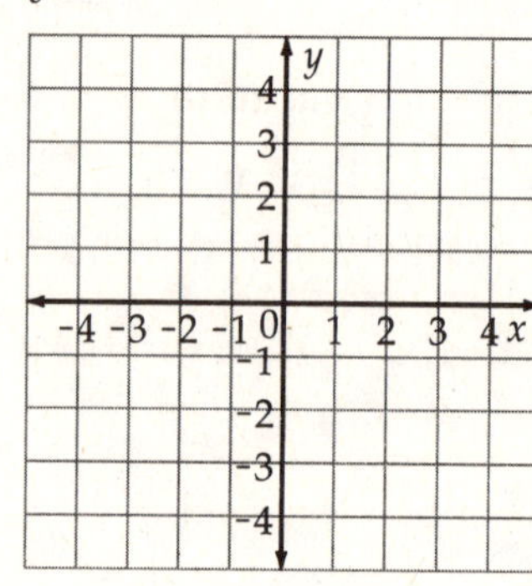

7. $x = -4$

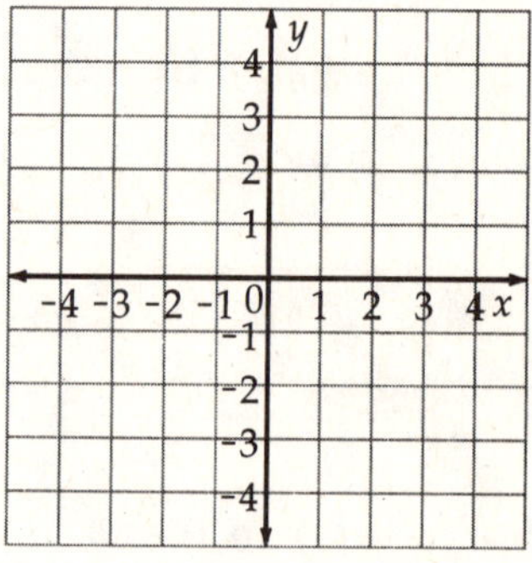

8. $y = 1.5$

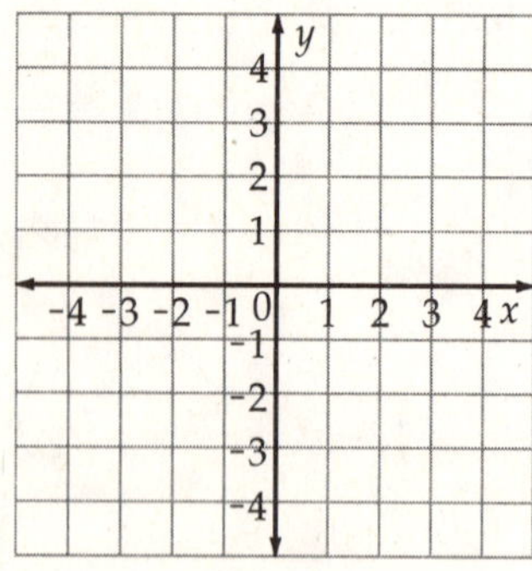

9. $3y = 2(x + 3)$

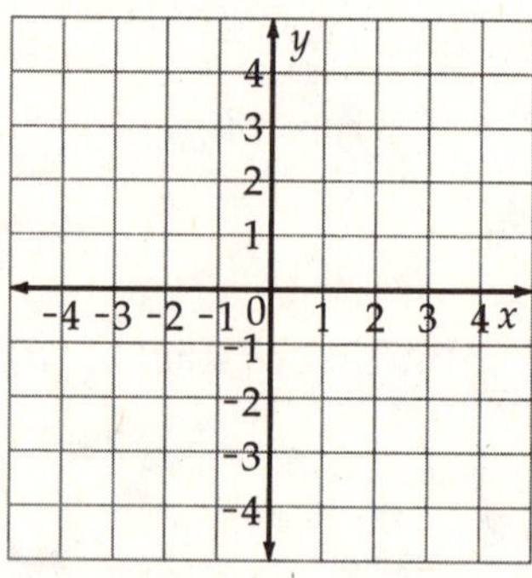

10. $x + y = 8(x + 1) - 4 + x$

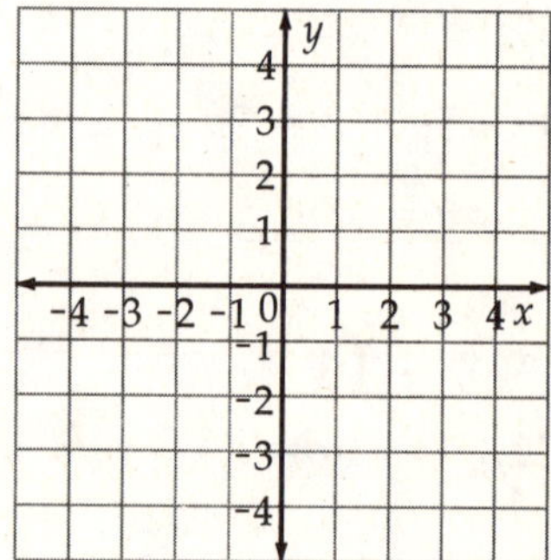

MENTAL MATH **Write an equation for each line described.**

11. the line 5 units above the x-axis _________

12. the line 3 units to the left of the line $x = -4$ _________

13. the line 6 units above the line $y = -8$ _________

14. the y-axis _________

Write an equation using two variables. Graph.

15. Find two numbers whose sum is 2. Equation: _______________

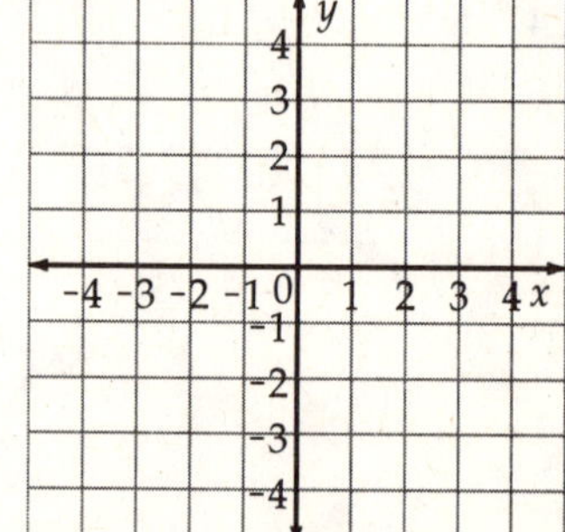

Practice

Slope and y-Intercept

Find the slope and *y*-intercept of each line.

1. 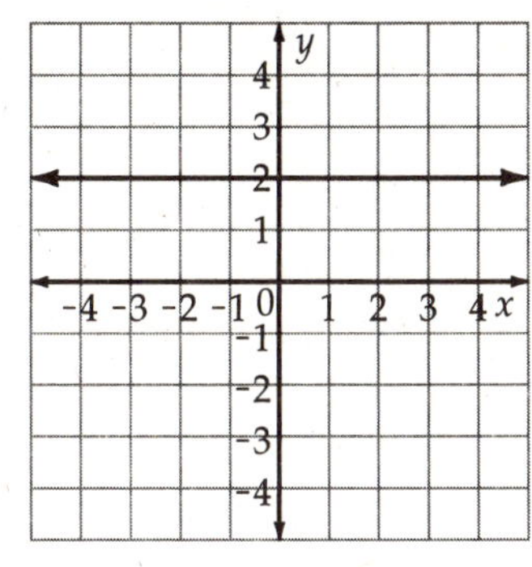

2. 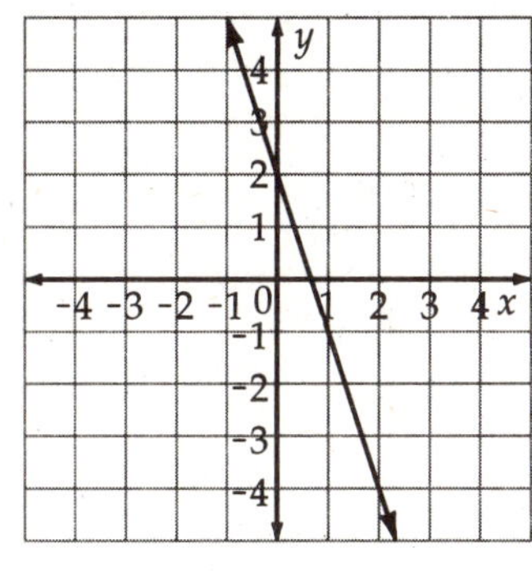

3. 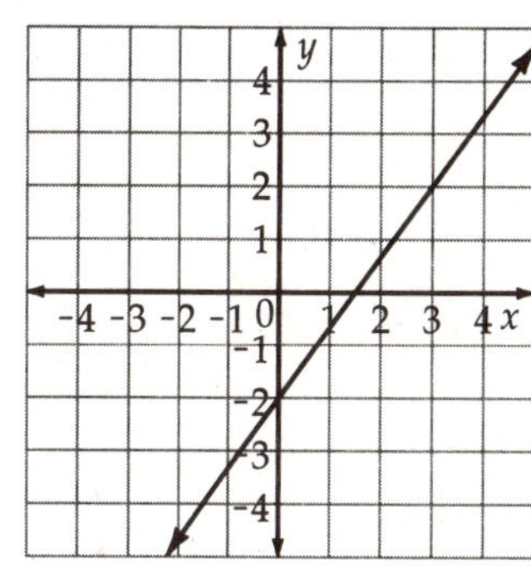

_____________   _____________   _____________

Find the slope of the line containing the given points.

4. $(1, 1), (6, 3)$ __________

5. $(-4, 6), (-4, 2)$ ______________

6. $(-8, -3), (4, -11)$ __________

7. $(3, -7), (-1, -7)$ __________

8. $(0, 9), (-5, -21)$ ______________

9. $(7, 2), (-1, 3)$ _________

Complete.

Equation	Equation in slope-intercept form	Slope	*y*-Intercept
10. $5x - y = 6$	_______________	_________	_________
11. $7x + 2y = 10$	_______________	_________	_________
12. $-x + 5y - 4 = 0$	_______________	_________	_________

On the coordinate axes, sketch the graph of each equation. Label the graph with the equation of the line.

13. $y = \frac{1}{4}x$ **14.** $2x + y = -2$ **15.** $6x - 4y = -12$

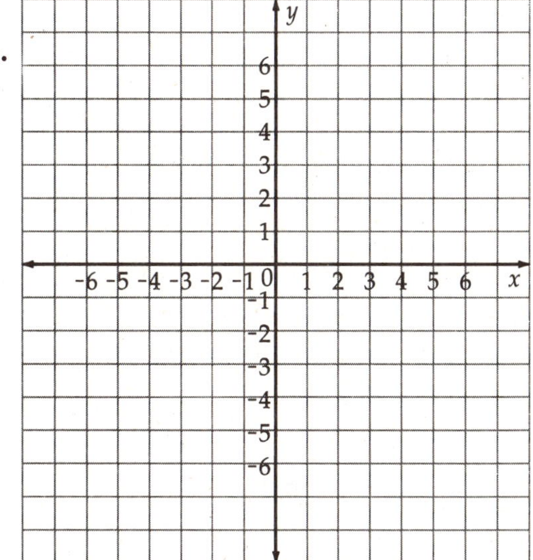

Write an equation in standard form for each line.

16. having slope -5 and *y*-intercept 6

____

17. passing through the points $(4, 0)$ and $(0, 3)$.

____

Practice

Solve by Graphing

Solve by using the strategy of graphing.

1. The water pressure at a depth of 100 ft in the ocean is 45 lb/ft^2. At a depth of 500 ft the pressure is 225 lb/ft^2.

   a. Graph this information.

   b. What is the approximate pressure at a depth of 800 ft?

   ____

   c. What is the approximate depth where the pressure is 180 lb/ft^2?

   ____

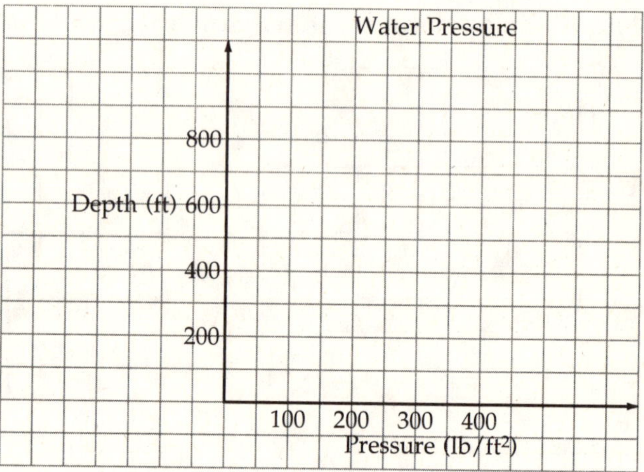

2. Tanya opened a savings account in 1984. She had $4,000 in the account by 1988 and $5,500 by 1991.

   a. Graph this information. Assume the value of the account increases constantly with time.

   b. What was the approximate amount in the account in 1986?

   ____

   c. About how much will be in the account in 1995?

   ____

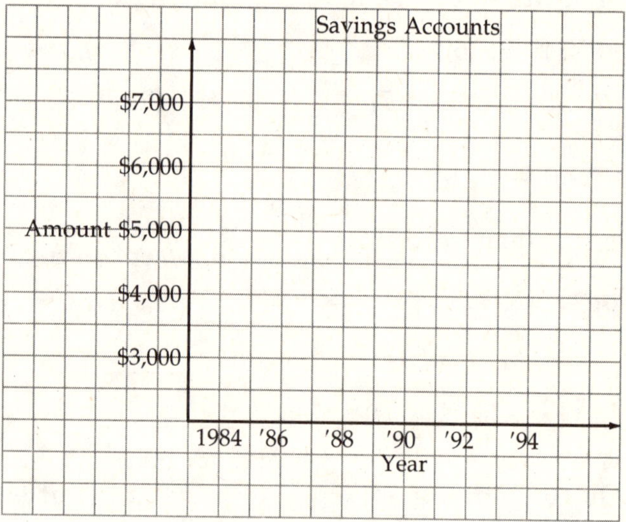

3. The driver of a car slowed to a stop at a constant rate. After 5 s the car was traveling 30 mi/h. After 8 s the car was traveling 12 mi/h.

   a. Graph this information.

   b. About how fast was the car moving when the driver first applied the brakes?

   ____

   c. About how long did it take the car to stop?

   ____

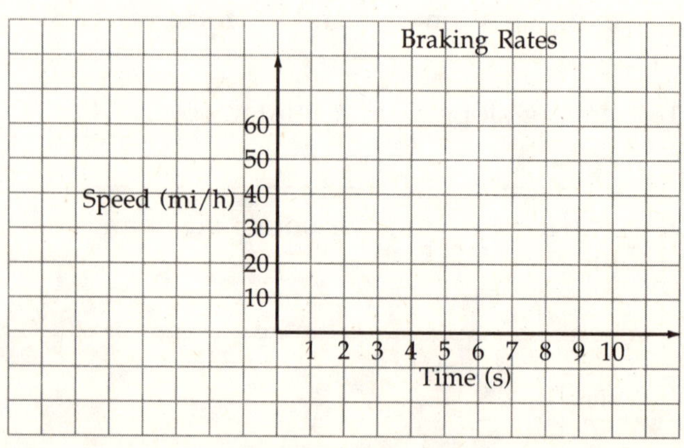

Chapter 8

Practice

Solving Systems of Linear Equations

Tell whether the ordered pair is a solution of the system. Write *yes* or *no*.

1. $y = 6x + 12$

$2x - y = 4$

$(-4, -12)$ _________

2. $y = -3x$

$x = 4y + \frac{1}{2}$

$\left(-\frac{1}{2}, \frac{3}{2}\right)$ _________

3. $x + 2y = 2$

$2x + 5y = 2$

$(6, -2)$ _________

Solve each system by graphing. Check your solutions.

4. $x + y = 3$

$x - y = -1$

Solution:

____

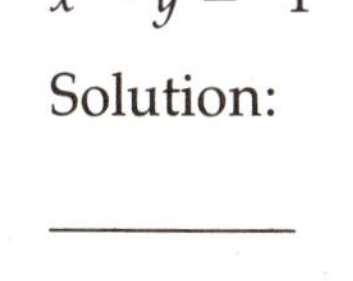
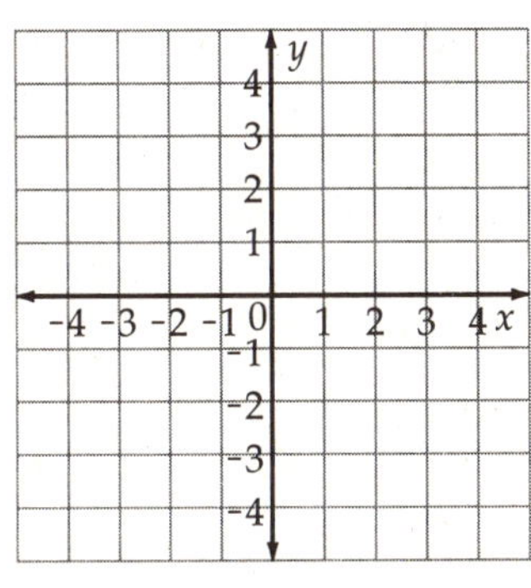

5. $2x + y = 1$

$x - 2y = 3$

Solution:

____

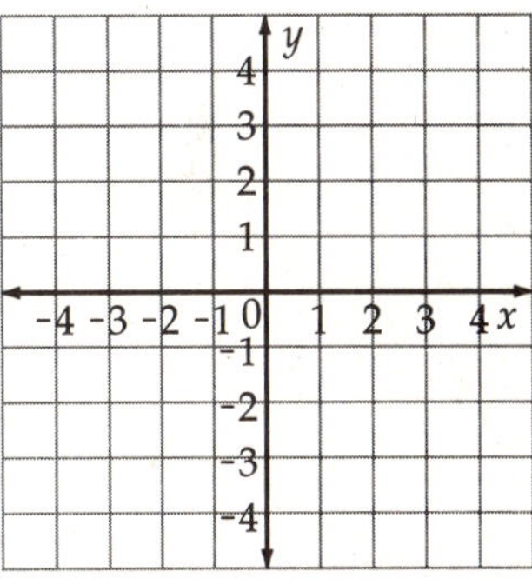

6. $y + 2 = 0$

$2x + y = 0$

Solution:

____

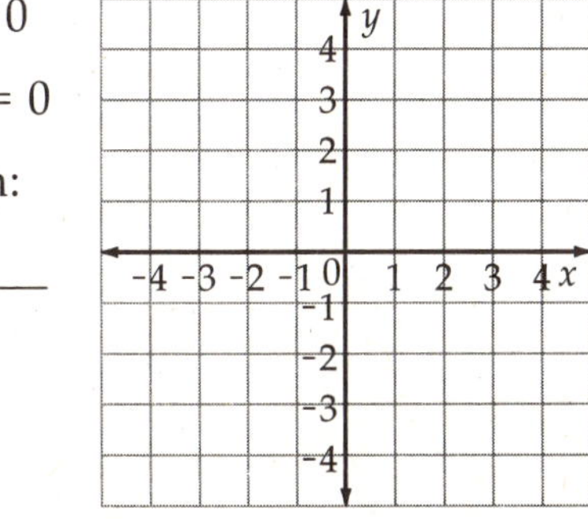

7. $3x + 2y = -6$

$x + 3y = -2$

Solution:

____

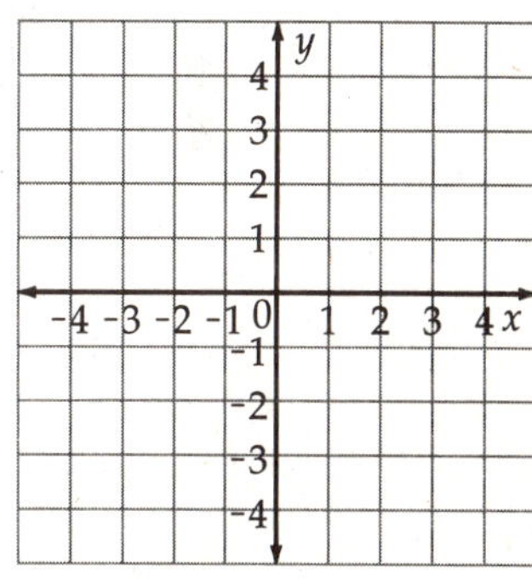

Write a system of linear equations. Solve by graphing.

8. The sum of two numbers is 3. Their difference is 1. Find the numbers.

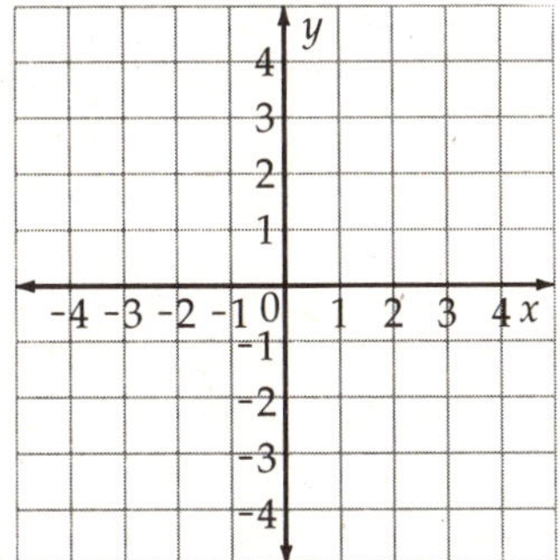

____

____

____

Practice

Solving Linear Inequalities

**Tell whether the ordered pair is a solution of the inequality.
Write *yes* or *no*.**

1. $-x + y \le 15$; (20, -5) _________

2. $x - 7y > 0$; (1, 4) _________

3. $x + 3y \le 9$; (3, 2) _________

4. $-5x - 4y > 6$; (-3, 2) _________

5. $|x - y| > 7$; (-4, 5) _________

6. $|x| - |y| > |x + y|$; (-15, 8) _________

7. $3x \ge 4y$; (-4, -3) _________

8. $2(5 - 3x) > -7y$; (5, 3) _________

CALCULATOR Tell whether the ordered pair is a solution of the
inequality. Write yes or no.

9. $3.2x - 4.67y > 0$; (1.04, -2.2) _________

10. $9.47x - 3.68y > 0$; (2.54, 7.16) _________

11. $4.8x \le 48 - 3.4y$; (-7.2, 3.6) _________

12. $|5.1x + 6.8y| \ge 50$; (-4.7, -3.9) _________

13. $4.9(8.2x - 12.6y) < 120$; (0.7, -1.5) _________

**Solve each inequality for y in terms of x. Write three ordered
pairs that are solutions of the inequality.**

14. $12x - 3y < 21$ _________________ ______ , ______ , ______

15. $x + 10 < 5y$ _________________ ______ , ______ , ______

16. $-2y + 8x \ge 22$ _________________ ______ , ______ , ______

17. $24 + 2(x - 3y) < 0$ _________________ ______ , ______ , ______

18. $\frac{3}{4}y > 9x + 12$ _________________ ______ , ______ , ______

19. $-6x + 3(7 - y) < -3$ _________________ ______ , ______ , ______

Joe spent less than $2.80 buying some $.25 stamps and some
$.20 stamps. Let x = the number of $.25 stamps he bought. Let
y = the number of $.20 stamps he bought.

20. Write an inequality describing Joe's purchase. _______________________

21. Solve the inequality for y in terms of x.

____

22. Find y for the given values of x.

    a. $x = 8$ _________

    b. $x = 4$ _________

Practice

Graphing Linear Inequalities

Write the equation of the line you would draw for each
inequality. Tell whether the graph of the equation would be
drawn as a solid or a dotted line. Write *solid* or *dotted*.

1. $4x - 5y \geq 3$ _______________________

2. $y < \frac{2}{3}x + 2$ _______________________

3. $2x > 3 - 2y$ _______________________

4. $y \leq -5$ _______________________

5. $-x + 2y > -3$ _______________________

6. $8 \leq 5y - 3x$ _______________________

Tell whether the region containing the origin would be shaded
in the graph of each inequality. Write yes or no.

7. $4x - 5y \geq 3$ _______

8. $y < \frac{2}{3}x + 2$ _______

9. $2x > 3 - 2y$ _______

10. $y \leq -5$ _______

11. $-x + 2y > -3$ _______

12. $8 \leq 5y - 3x$ _______

Graph each inequality.

13. $y < x$

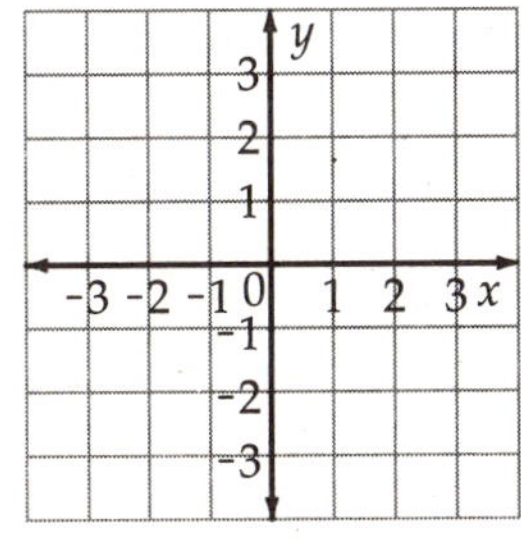

14. $x + y < 2$

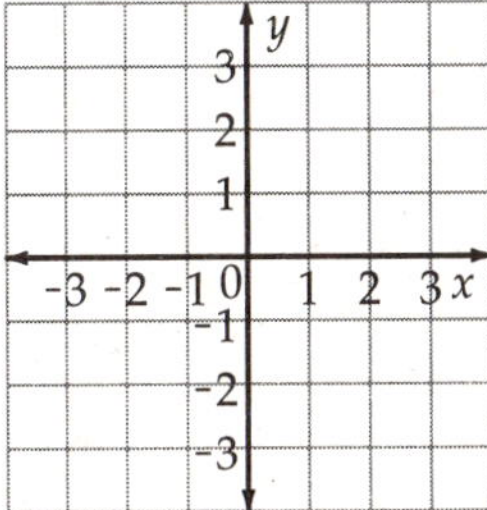

15. $y \leq x - 1$

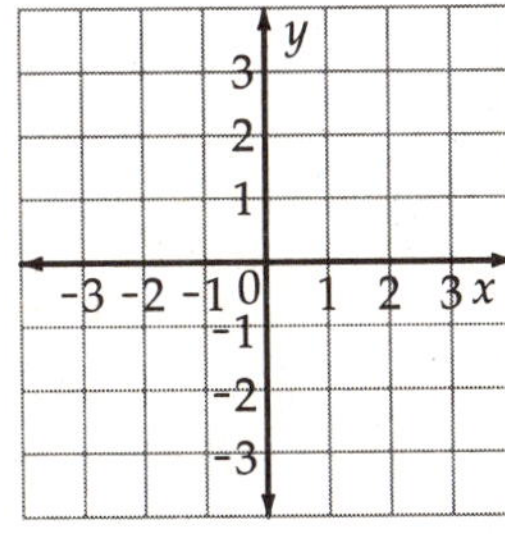

16. $x > -2$

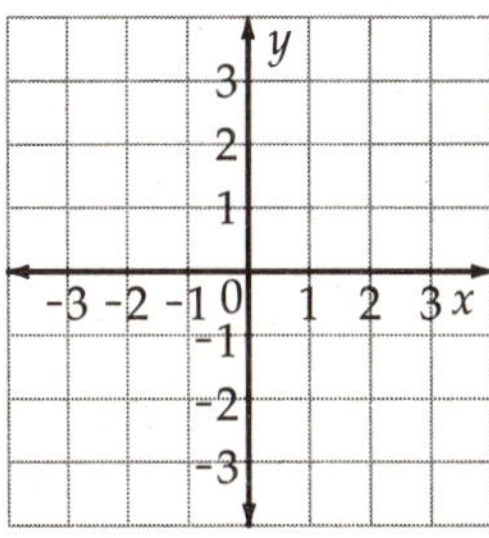

17. $-3x \geq 6 - 2y$

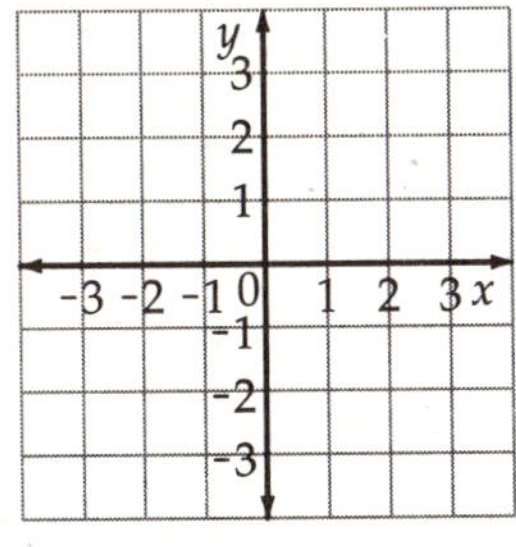

18. $x + 2y \geq 4$

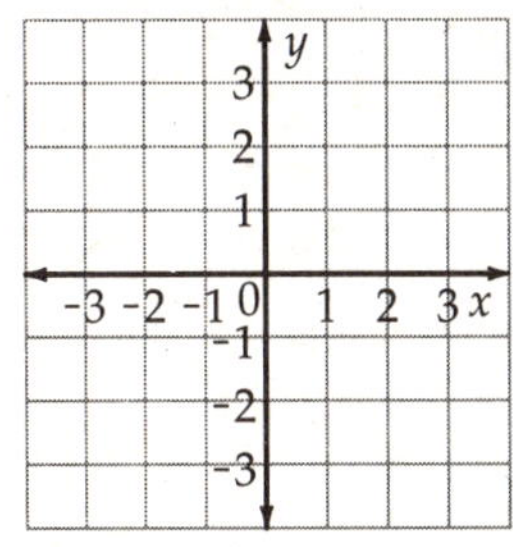

Practice

Introduction to Geometry

Complete. Use *point, line, plane, segment,* or *ray*.

1. A ___________ continues without end in opposite directions.

2. A ___________ is part of a line and has two endpoints.

3. A ___________ represents a position in space.

4. A ___________ is a flat surface with no thickness.

5. A ___________ is part of a line and has one endpoint.

True **or** *false?*

6. Parallel lines lie in the same plane. ________

7. Skew lines may be parallel. ________

8. $\overleftrightarrow{AB}$ and $\overleftrightarrow{CB}$ name the same line. ________

9. $\overrightarrow{AB}$ and $\overrightarrow{BA}$ name the same ray. ________

10. $\overrightarrow{AB}$ and $\overrightarrow{AC}$ name the same ray. ________

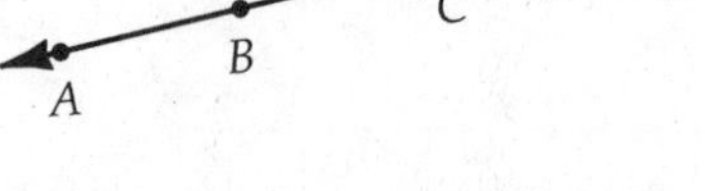

11. Name all possible segments in the figure.

____

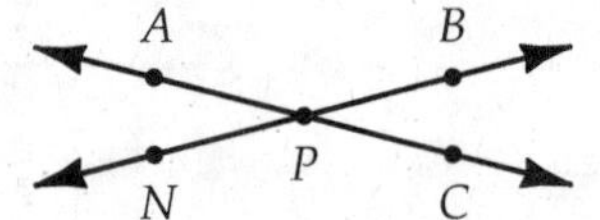

12. Name a line containing N and B. ____

13. How do you know that $\overleftrightarrow{AC}$ and $\overleftrightarrow{NB}$ are not parallel?

____

Complete, using the three-dimensional figure. Use parallel lines, skew lines, parallel planes, or intersecting planes.

14. $\overleftrightarrow{AD}$ and $\overleftrightarrow{EH}$ are ___________________________.

15. $ABCD$ and $AEFB$ are ___________________________.

16. $\overleftrightarrow{EF}$ and $\overleftrightarrow{AD}$ are ___________________________.

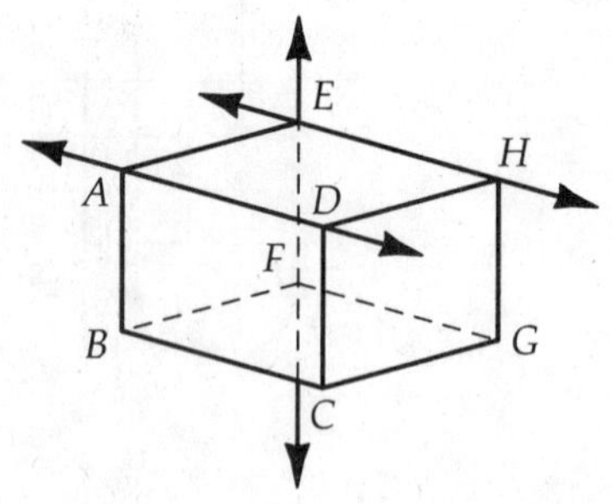

Find the length of the indicated segments.

17. 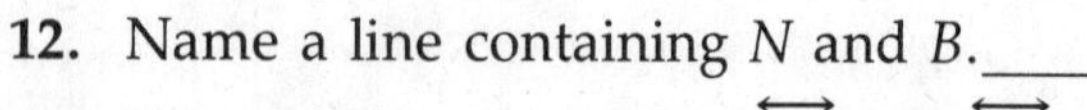

$AB =$ ___________ $AC =$ ___________

18. 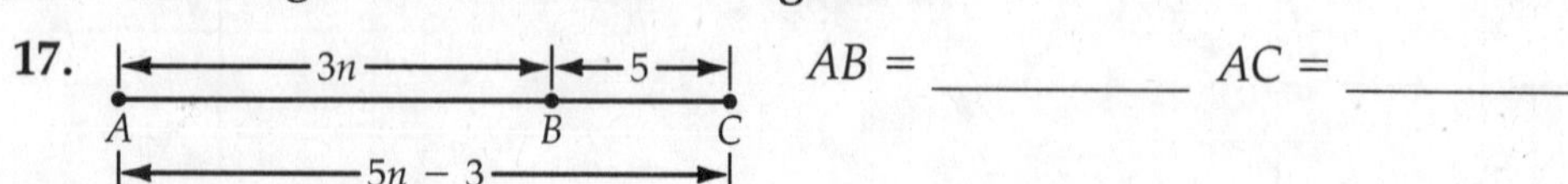

$KL =$ ___________ $MN =$ ___________ $KN =$ ___________

Practice

Angles

Classify each angle as acute, obtuse, right, or straight.

1. 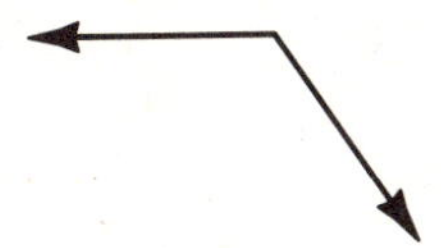 **2.** 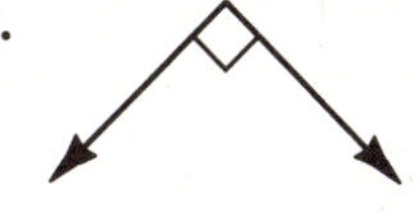 **3.**  **4.** 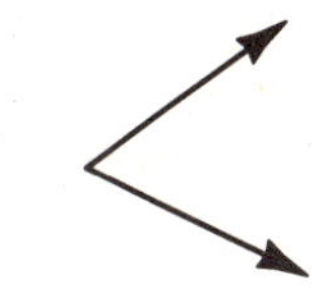

_______ _______ _______ _______

Name the angle that forms a vertical angle with the angle named.

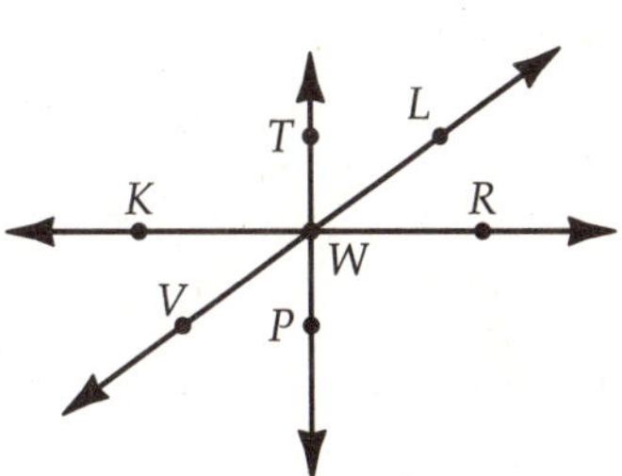

5. $\angle RWP$ _______ **6.** $\angle KWV$ _______

7. $\angle TWL$ _______

Find the measure of each indicated angle.

8. $m\angle ABD$ _______

  $m\angle DBC$ _______

9. $m\angle RNP$ _______

  $m\angle QNP$ _______

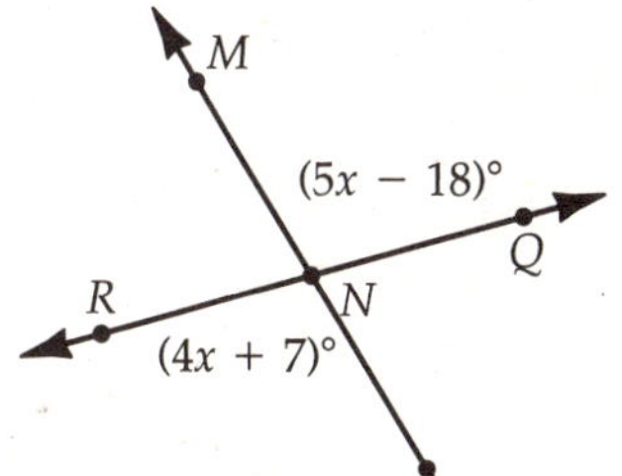

Use a protractor to find the measure of each angle.

10. 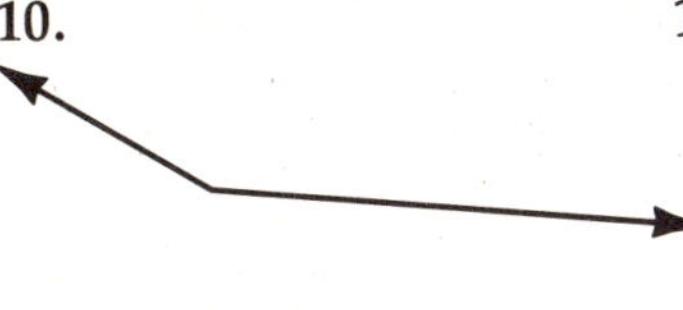 **11.** 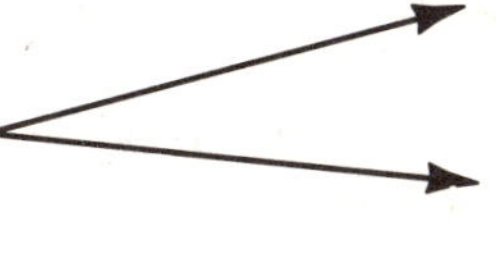 **12.** 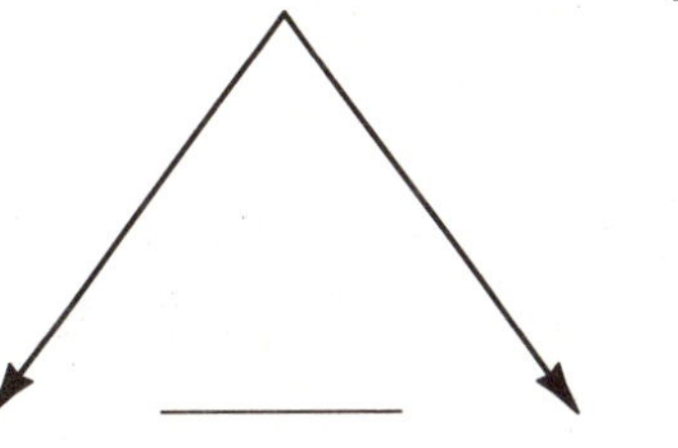

_______ _______ _______

Complete.

	Measure of Angle	Acute, Right, Obtuse, or Straight	Measure of Supplement	Measure of Complement (if possible)
13.	21°	_______	_______	_______
14.	119°	_______	_______	_______
15.	178°	_______	_______	_______
16.	57.6°	_______	_______	_______

17. Find a pair of complementary angles such that the difference

  of their measures is 12°. _________________________________

Practice

Polygons and Quadrilaterals

Is the figure a polygon? Write *yes* or *no*.

1. 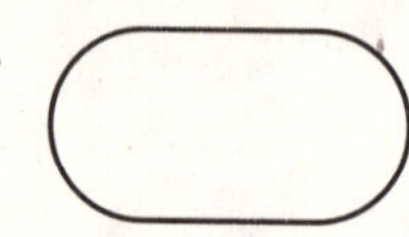

2. 

3. 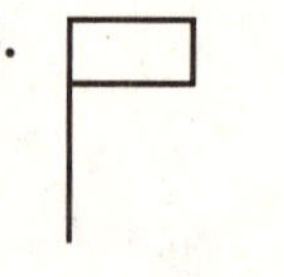

_______________   _______________   _______________

Tell whether the statement is *true* or *false*.

4. A quadrilateral is a polygon with four sides. _________

5. All quadrilaterals are parallelograms. _________

6. A rhombus is an equilateral parallelogram. _________

7. A square is a rectangle. _________

8. No trapezoid is a parallelogram. _________

9. All squares are convex polygons. _________

Give two other correct names for each figure.

10. 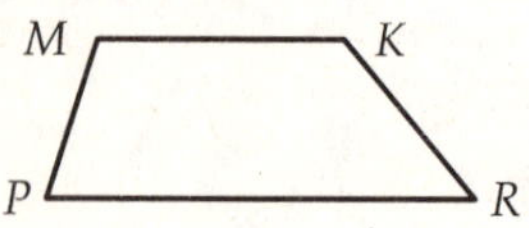

trapezoid *PMKR* _____________________

11. 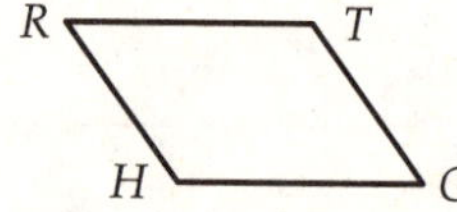

parallelogram *RTGH* _____________________

Write whether the polygon is concave or convex. Then classify the polygon by the number of sides.

12. 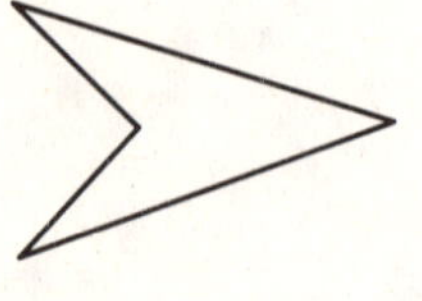

13. 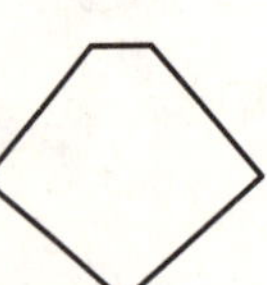

14. 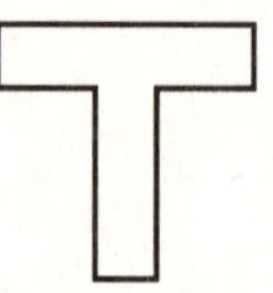

_______________   _______________   _______________

_______________   _______________   _______________

Draw a figure to fit each description.

15. convex hexagon   16. triangle   17. concave quadrilateral

Practice

Triangles

Classify each triangle by its angles or its sides.

1. 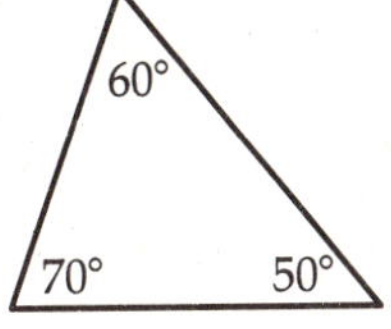

____

2. 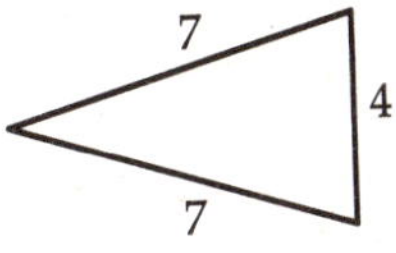

____

3. 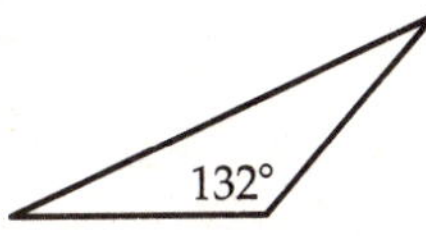

____

4. 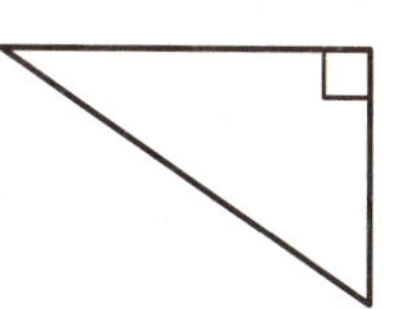

____

5. 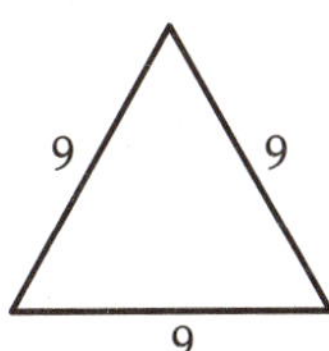

____

6. 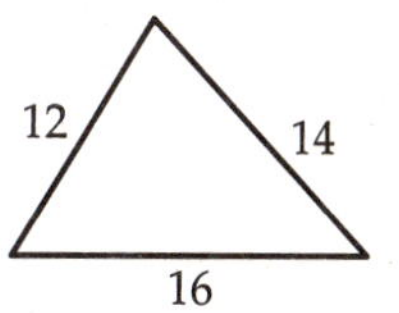

____

Tell whether the statement is *true* or *false*.

7. An equilateral triangle is isosceles. _________

8. A triangle can have more than one right angle. _________

9. A scalene triangle may be isosceles. _________

10. An equilateral triangle cannot be obtuse. _________

11. A right triangle may be an acute triangle. _________

12. A triangle cannot have more than one obtuse angle. _________

Find the measure of the indicated angle.

13. 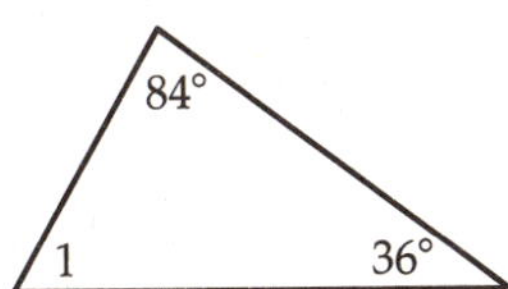

$m\angle 1 =$ _________

14. 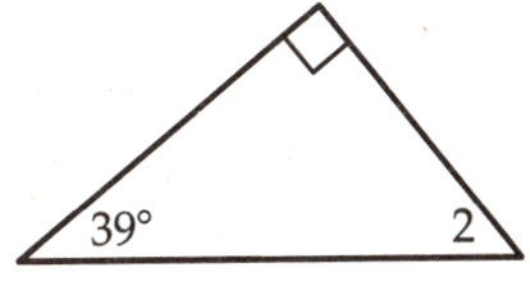

$m\angle 2 =$ _________

15. 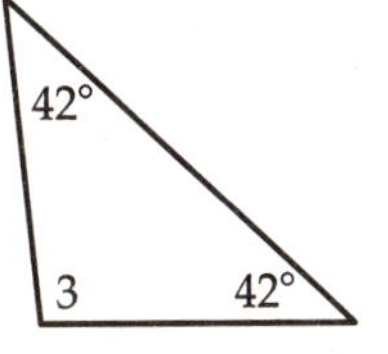

$m\angle 3 =$ _________

CALCULATOR Find the measure of the third angle of a triangle
that has two angles with the given measures.

16. 117°, 58° _________   **17.** 9°, 23° _________   **18.** 155.5°, 23° _________

19. The measures of the angles of a triangle are $(3x + 15)°$,
$(4x - 21)°$, and $(2x + 24)°$. Find the measure of each angle.

____

Practice

Circles

True or *false?*

1. All chords of a circle pass through the center. _________

2. A diameter of a circle has length twice that of a radius. _________

3. A diameter is a chord. _________

4. All radii of a circle have the same length. _________

5. The center of a circle is part of the circle. _________

MENTAL MATH **For each length, find the radius or the diameter.**

6. $d = 60$ m

   $r =$ _________

7. $r = 12.5$ in.

   $d =$ _________

8. $r = 35$ yd

   $d =$ _________

9. $d = 2{,}400$ mm

   $r =$ _________

10. $r = 90$ ft

    $d =$ _________

11. $d = 500$ m

    $r =$ _________

CALCULATOR **For each length, find the radius or the diameter.**

12. $r = 38.9$ cm

    $d =$ _________

13. $d = 0.77$ m

    $r =$ _________

14. $r = 587.9$ m

    $d =$ _________

15. $r = 64{,}395$ in.

    $d =$ _________

16. $d = 1{,}365$ ft

    $r =$ _________

17. $d = 147{,}681$ km

    $r =$ _________

Name the indicated part of circle O.

18. $\overline{MK}$ _________

19. $\overline{OP}$ _________

20. $\overline{MP}$ _________

21. $\angle KOP$ _________

22. What kind of triangle is $\triangle OMK$? _________

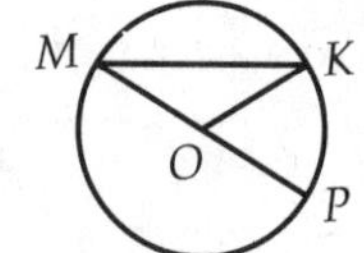

23. Use the data to construct a circle graph.

Voter Preference for Senator

Peterson	40%
Washington	30%
Gomex	15%
Thomson	10%
Miller	5%

Practice

Congruence and Symmetry

Circle the figure that does not appear to be congruent to the other three.

1. 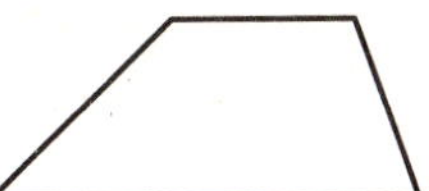 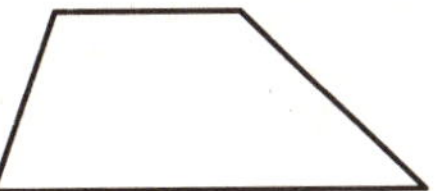 

2. 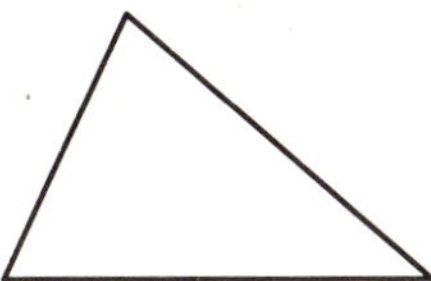 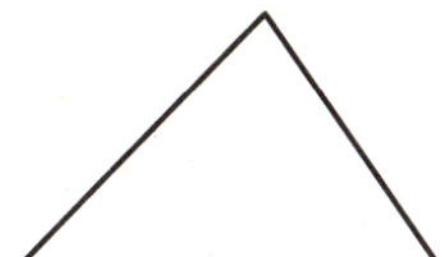 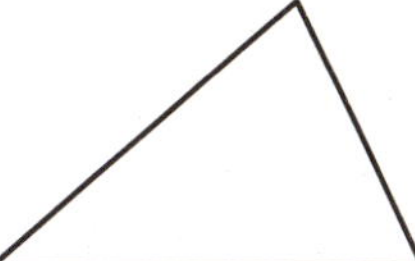 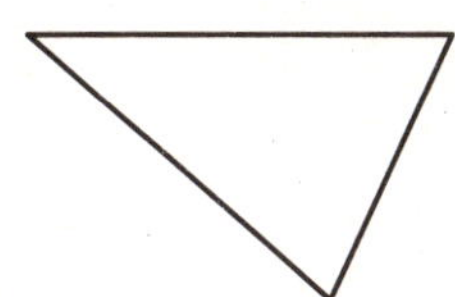

$\triangle GHM \cong \triangle RSA$. **Complete.**

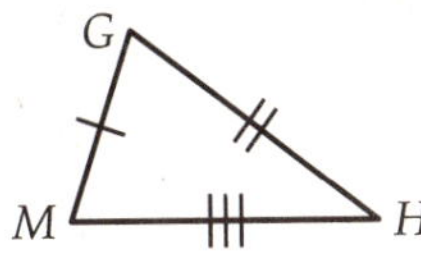 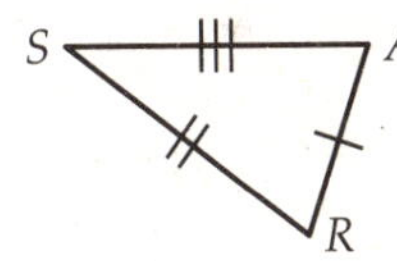

3. $\overline{GH} \cong$ ________

4. $\overline{AS} \cong$ ________

5. $\angle S \cong$ ________

6. $\angle M \cong$ ________

7. $\overline{AR} \cong$ ________

8. $\angle R \cong$ ________

HPKT $\cong$ *BEWL*. **Complete.**

9. $\overline{PK} \cong$ ________

10. $\angle L \cong$ ________

11. $\angle KPH \cong$ ________

12. $\overline{LB} \cong$ ________

13. $\overline{EB} \cong$ ________

14. $\angle PHT \cong$ ________

Find the measure of the indicated angle.

15. $\triangle ABC \cong \triangle MNP$

   a. $m\angle B =$ ________

   b. $m\angle M =$ ________

   c. $m\angle N =$ ________

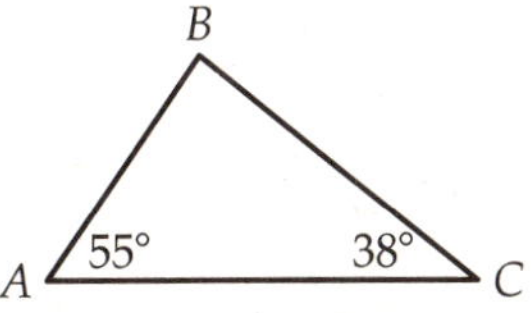 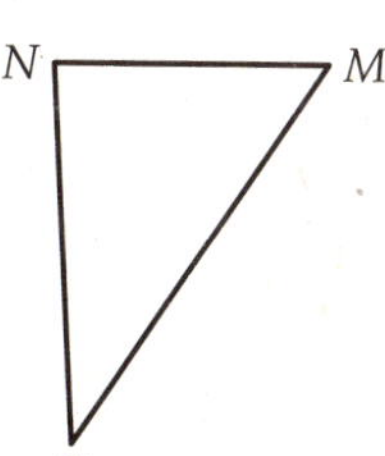

Is the dotted line a line of symmetry? Write *yes* or *no*.

16. 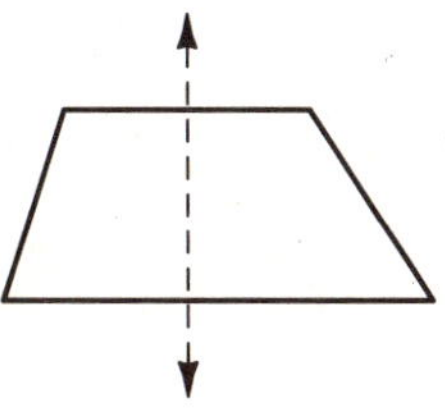

____

17. 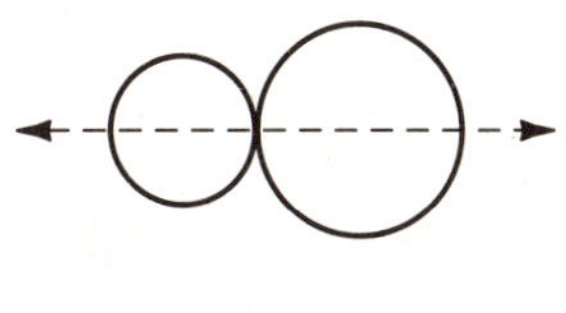

____

18. 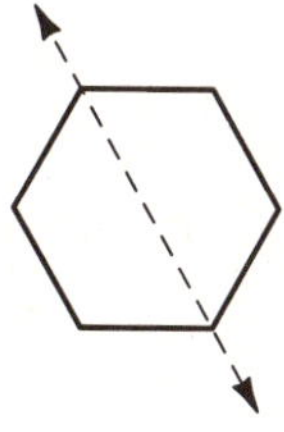

____

Practice

Similar Figures

Sketch a figure similar to, but not congruent to, each figure.

1. 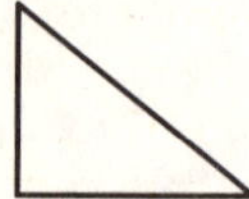

2. 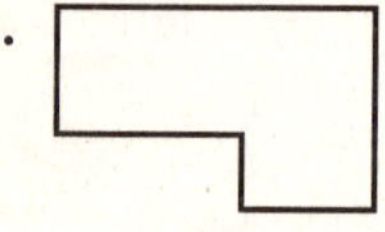

KLSN ~ PAGT. Complete each proportion.

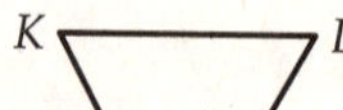
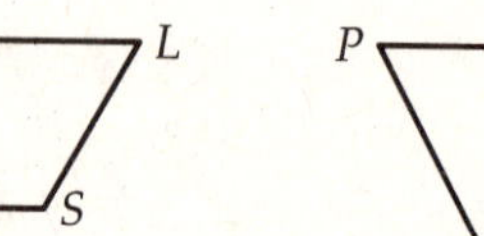
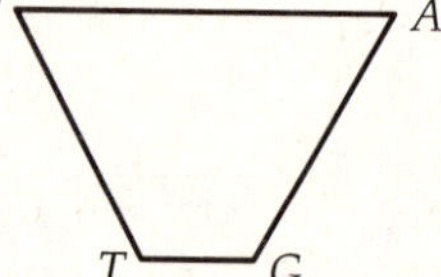

3. $\dfrac{LS}{AG} = \dfrac{?}{PT}$ _______

4. $\dfrac{LK}{?} = \dfrac{SL}{GA}$ _______

5. $\dfrac{TG}{NS} = \dfrac{PA}{?}$ _______

6. $\dfrac{?}{NS} = \dfrac{PT}{KN}$ _______

Assume each pair of triangles is similar. Find x and y.

7. $x =$ _______

$y =$ _______

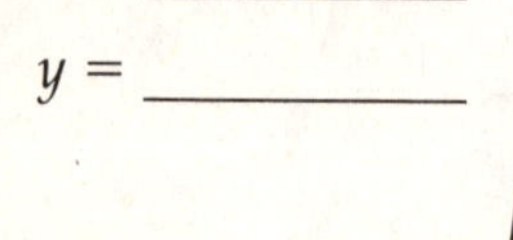
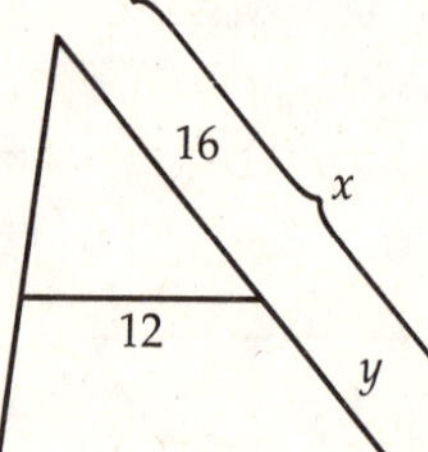

8. $x =$ _______

$y =$ _______

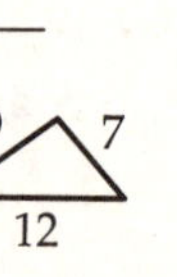
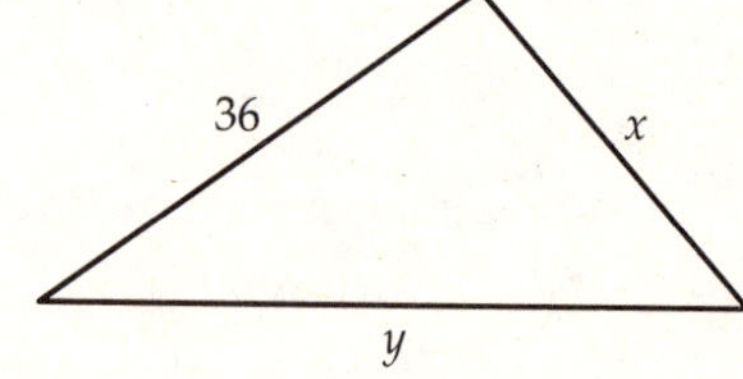

Solve.

9. A rectangular painting is 56 in. long and 36 in. wide. A photo of the painting is 4.5 in. wide. How long is the photo?

____

10. At the same time a lighthouse casts a 99-ft shadow, a 24-ft telephone pole casts a 54-ft shadow. How tall is the lighthouse?

____

Practice

Perimeter and Circumference

Find the perimeter of each figure.

1. a rectangle with length 17 in. and width 9 in. _____________

2. an isosceles triangle with base 11.3 cm and sides 14.2 cm _____________

3. a scalene triangle with sides 2 ft 4 in., 3 ft 5 in., and 4 ft 6 in. _____________

Find the perimeter of each polygon.

4.
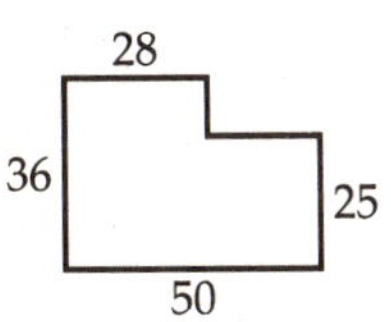

5.
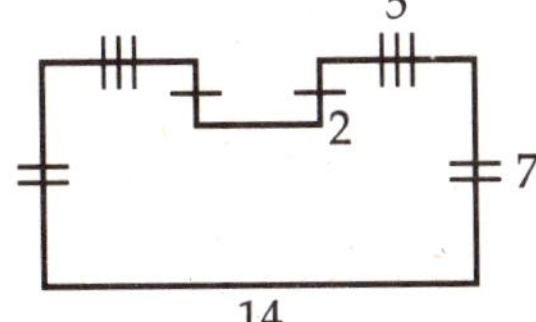

6.
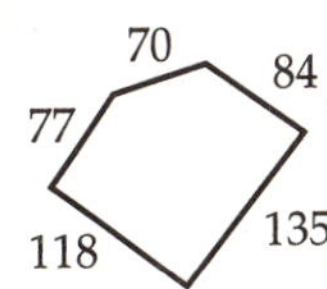

_____________   _____________   _____________

Find the circumference of each figure. Use 3.14 for π.

7.
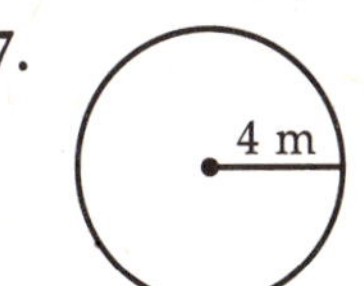

8.
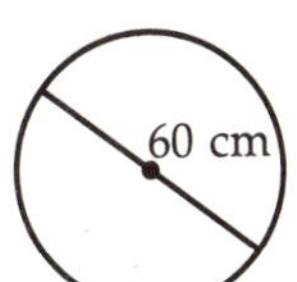

9.
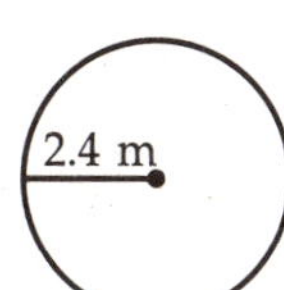

10.
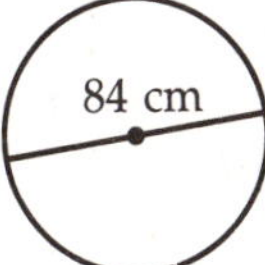

_____________   _____________   _____________   _____________

Find the diameter and radius of a circle with the given circumference.

11. $C = 8\pi$ in. $d =$ _____________

     $r =$ _____________

12. $C = 56.2\pi$ cm $d =$ _____________

     $r =$ _____________

CALCULATOR Find the circumference to the nearest tenth of a unit. Use 3.14 for π.

13. $d = 25.8$

     $C =$ _____________

14. $r = 9.1$

     $C =$ _____________

15. $r = 0.07$

     $C =$ _____________

Find the circumference. Use $\frac{22}{7}$ for π.

16. $d = 14$

     $C =$ _____________

17. $d = 1\frac{3}{11}$

     $C =$ _____________

18. $r = \frac{7}{8}$

     $C =$ _____________

19. A rectangle with length 17.3 cm has perimeter 46.8 cm. Find the width.

____

Practice

Draw a Diagram

Solve using a diagram. Use 3.14 for π.

1. An old-fashioned "high-wheel" bicycle had a small wheel with diameter 8 in. in back and a large wheel with diameter 56 in. in front. A circular bicycle track had diameter 112 ft.

   a. Find the circumference in inches.

   back wheel _______________ front wheel _______________ track _______________

   b. Find the number of complete wheel revolutions in one circuit of the track.

   back wheel _______________ front wheel _______________

   c. A rider made 100 circuits of the track. How many more revolutions did the back wheel make than the front?

   ____

2. Two runners ran once around the track, one on the very inside, one on the very outside. How much farther did the outside runner run than the inside runner did? (Hint: Use 120 ft as a radius.)

   ____

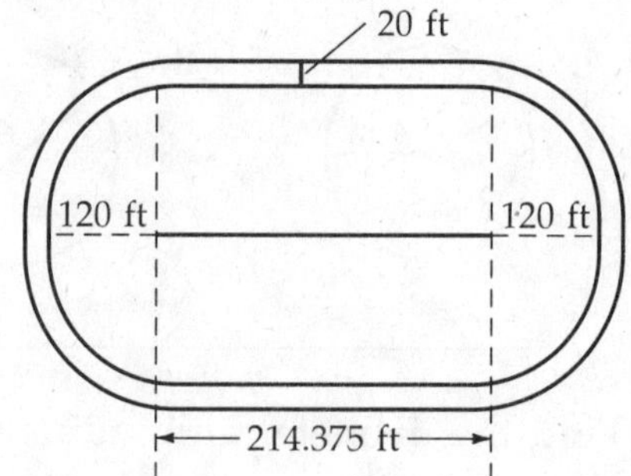

3. A circular lighthouse has radius 10 m. A circular fence around the outside of the lighthouse has circumference 12.56 m greater than that of the lighthouse.

   a. Find the circumference of the lighthouse. _______________

   b. Find the circumference of the fence. _______________

   c. Calculate the radius of the fence. _______________

   d. How far is the fence from the lighthouse? _______________

4. To make a pencil holder, Maria tied pieces of colored string around the outside of a cylindrical can 4 in. in diameter and 6 in. high. The string was $\frac{1}{12}$ in. in diameter. Maria used 1 in. of string to tie each knot. How much string did she use if she covered the entire outside of the can with circles of string?

   ____

5. Four circular pies fit exactly into a square box measuring 18 in. on a side. Find the circumference of one of the pies.

   ____

Practice

Area of Rectangles and Parallelograms

CALCULATOR **Find the area of each figure.**

1. 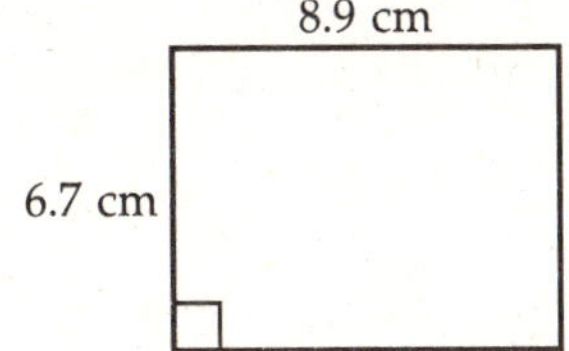

2. 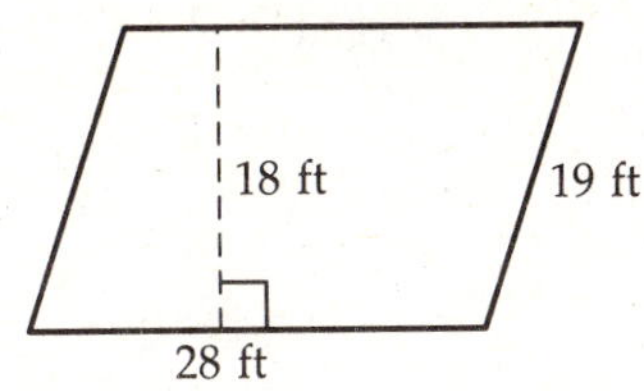

3. 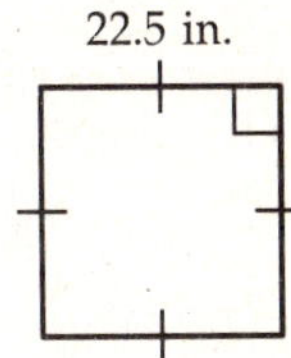

4. 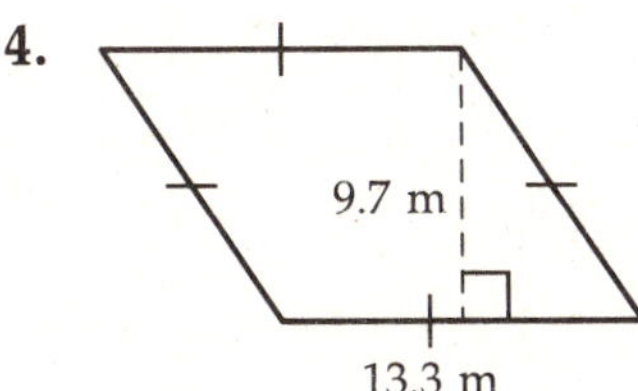

5. 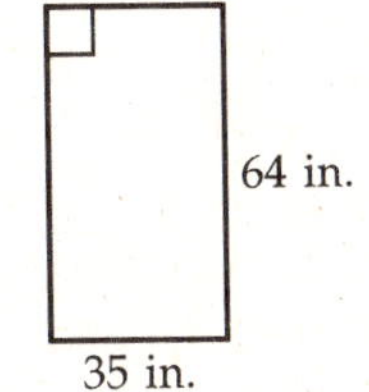

6. 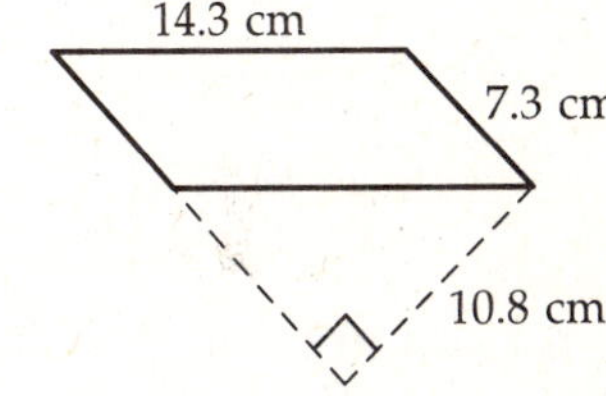

Find the missing measures.

7. A parallelogram
Area = 133 in.^{2}
$b = 19$ in.

$h =$ _________

8. A rectangle
Area = 76.56 cm^2
$h = 8.8$ cm

$b =$ _________

9. A parallelogram
Area = 96 km^2
$h = 12$ km

$b =$ _________

Find the area for the given rectangles or parallelograms. Use a calculator where necessary. Round to the nearest hundredth.

10. $l = 5.09$ m, $w = 4.3$ m _____________

11. $l = 35.5$ mi, $w = 8.25$ mi _____________

12. $l = 14x$, $w = 9$ _____________

13. $l = x + 5$, $w = 24$ _____________

14. $b = 84$ in., $h = 67$ in. _____________

15. $b = 0.094$ cm, $h = 0.07$ cm _____________

16. $b = x + 4x$, $h = 9x - 6x$ _____________

17. $b = 2x - 7$, $h = 8$ _____________

18. The area of a rectangle is 156 yd^2. The length is 13 yd. What is its perimeter?

____

19. The perimeter of a square is 72 in. What is its area?

____

20. Surveyors sometimes measure in links and rods. There are 25 links in a rod. How many square links are in a square rod?

____

Practice

Area of Triangles and Trapezoids

Find the area of each triangle.

1. base = 24 in.
height = 9 in.

area = _______________

2. height = 2.7 cm
base = 3.4 cm

area = _______________

3. base = 40 ft
height = 8.25 ft

area = _______________

4.

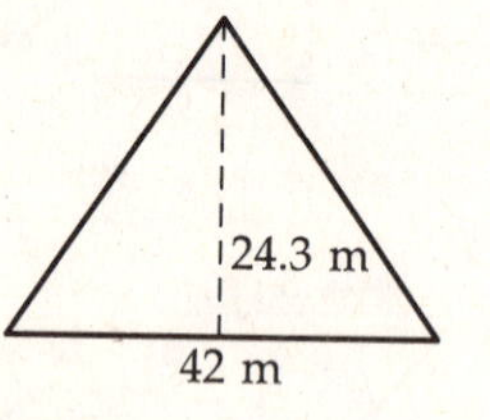

area = _______________

5.

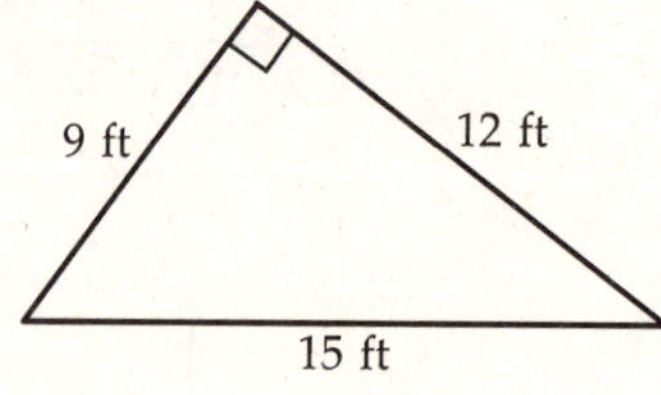

area = _______________

6.

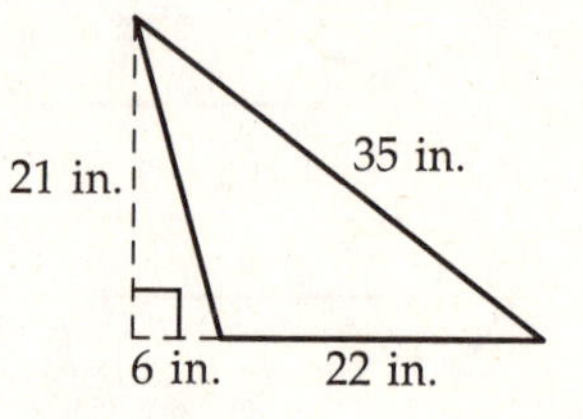

area = _______________

Find the area of each trapezoid.

7. $base_1$ = 13 in.
$base_2$ = 8 in.
height = 5 in.

area = _______________

8. $base_1$ = 24.6 cm
$base_2$ = 9.4 cm
height = 15.8 cm

area = _______________

9. height = 3.5 ft
$base_1$ = 2.25 ft
$base_2$ = 4.5 ft

area = _______________

10.

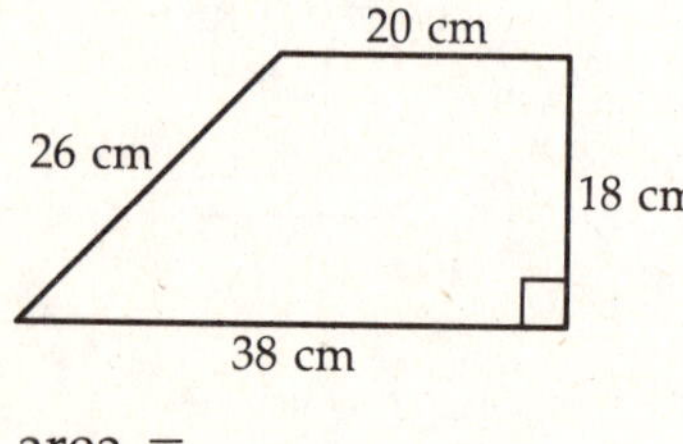

area = _______________

11.

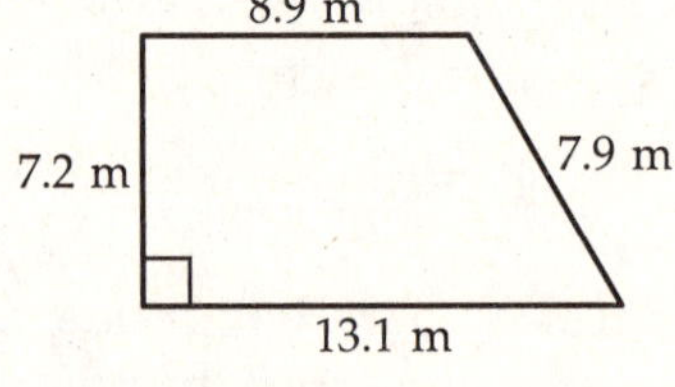

area = _______________

12.

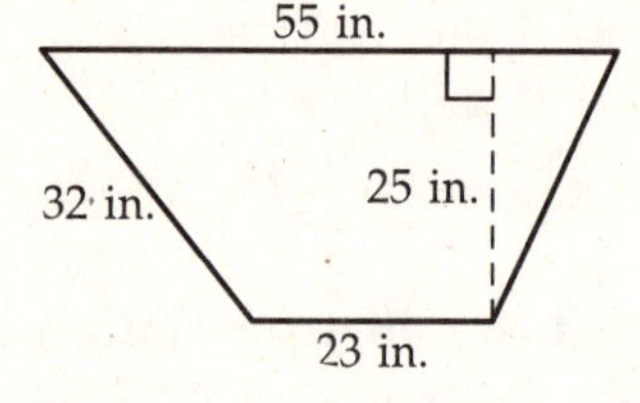

area = _______________

Find the missing values.

	Figure	Height	Base$_1$	Base$_2$	Area
13.	trapezoid	0.7 m	0.44 m	0.59 m	
14.	triangle	6.5 cm	9.9 cm		
15.	triangle	18 in.			63 in.²
16.	trapezoid		25 m	34 m	354 m²

17. a. Find the area of the triangle. __________

b. Find x. __________

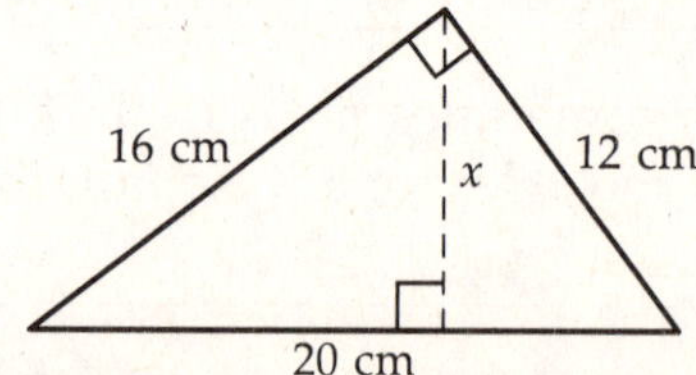

Practice

Area of Circles

Find the area of each circle. Give an exact answer and an approximate answer. Use 3.14 for π.

1. $r = 7$ m

$A =$ _______________________

$A \approx$ _______________________

2. $d = 18$ cm

$A =$ _______________________

$A \approx$ _______________________

3. $d = 42$ m

$A =$ _______________________

$A \approx$ _______________________

4. $r = 35$ km

$A =$ _______________________

$A \approx$ _______________________

5. $d = 22$ cm

$A =$ _______________________

$A \approx$ _______________________

6. $r = 25$ ft

$A =$ _______________________

$A \approx$ _______________________

7.

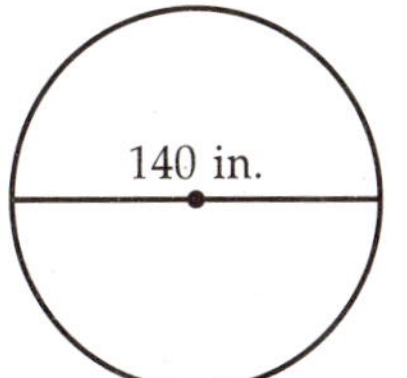

$A =$ _______________________

$A \approx$ _______________________

8.

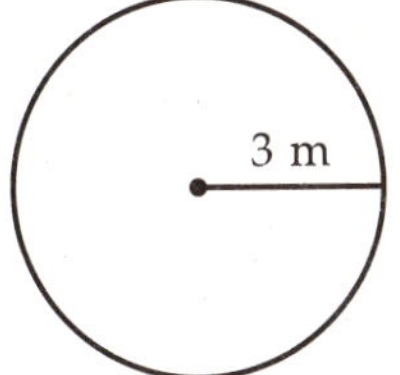

$A =$ _______________________

$A \approx$ _______________________

9.

$A =$ _______________________

$A \approx$ _______________________

10. $d = 8x$

$A =$ _______________________

$A \approx$ _______________________

11. $r = 10x$

$A =$ _______________________

$A \approx$ _______________________

12. $r = 2y$

$A =$ _______________________

$A \approx$ _______________________

Find the radius of each circle.

13. $A = 144\pi$ ft^2

$r =$ _______________________

14. $A = 676\pi$ cm^2

$r =$ _______________________

15. $A = 3{,}600\pi$ km^2

$r =$ _______________________

Find the circumference and area of each circle. Give an exact answer.

16. $r = 13$ in.

$C =$ _______________________

$A =$ _______________________

17. $d = 46$ ft

$C =$ _______________________

$A =$ _______________________

18. $r = 5kx$

$C =$ _______________________

$A =$ _______________________

19. A circle has a circumference of 78π yd. What is the area of the circle?

____

20. Circle 1 has a radius of 12 in. Circle 2 has a radius of 24 in. Find the ratio of the area of the smaller circle to the area of the larger. _______________________

Practice

For use after 10-4 (pp. 420–423)

Space Figures

Name each space figure.

1. 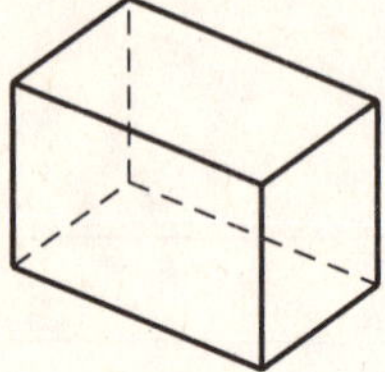

2. 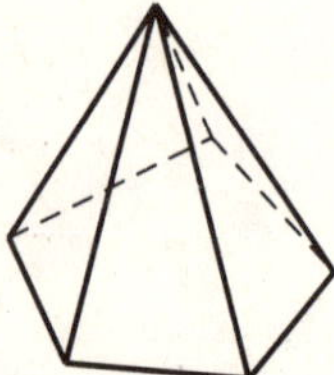

3. 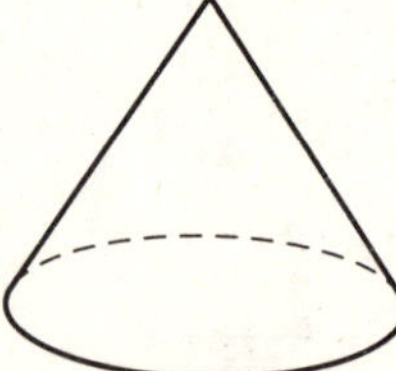

____

4. 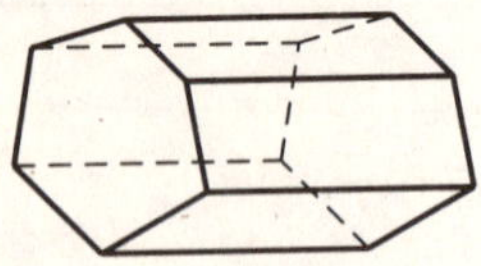

5. 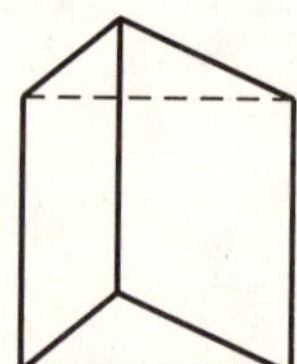

6. 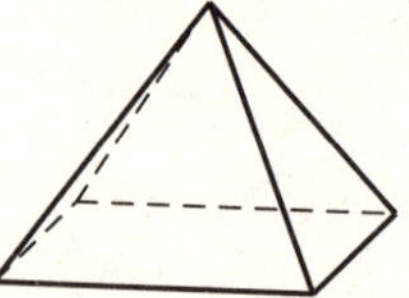

____

Complete by naming the missing polygon.

7. Each side of a triangular prism is a _______________________________

8. The base of a heptagonal pyramid is a _______________________________

9. Each side of a rectangle-based pyramid is a _______________________________

10. Each side of a trapezoidal prism is a _______________________________

11. Each base of a hexagonal prism is a _______________________________

Name the space figure that can be formed from each net.

12. 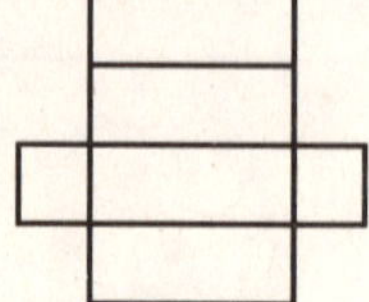

13. 

14. 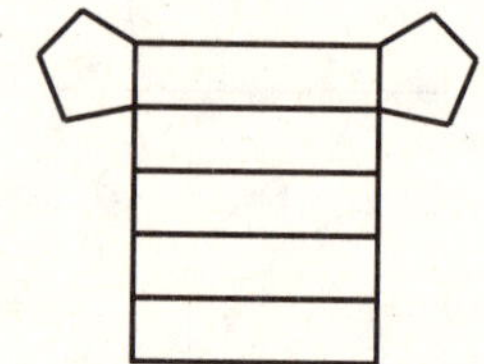

____

15. Name the number and types of polygons that form the faces of a hexagonal prism.

____

16. Name the number and types of polygons that form the faces of a hexagonal pyramid.

____

Chapter 10

Practice

Make a Model

1. Eighty phone numbers are chosen at random from a telephone book.

   a. Guess approximately how many numbers will end in 3, 4, or 5.

   ____

   b. Conduct an experiment, choosing 80 numbers from a phone book. How many end in 3, 4, or 5?

   ____

   ____

2. A narrow strip of paper is twisted once, then joined at the ends with glue or tape. The strip is then cut lengthwise along the dotted line shown.

   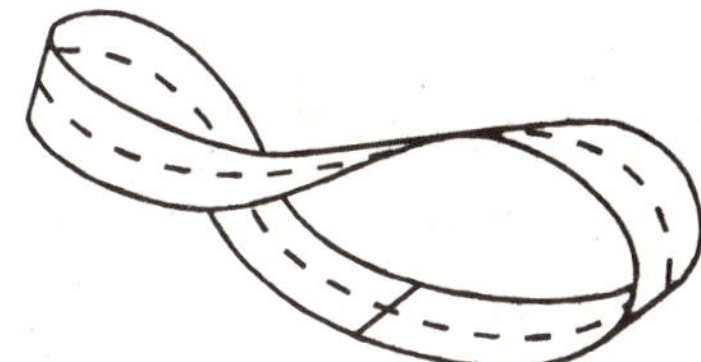

   a. Guess the results.

   ____

   b. Make and cut a model as directed. What are the results?

   ____

3. The midpoint of a segment is the point that divides the segment into two segments of equal length. A quadrilateral with unequal sides is drawn. The midpoints of the four sides are found and connected in order.

   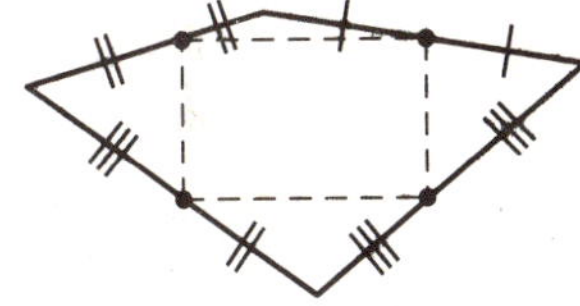

   a. Guess what kind of quadrilateral is formed.

   ____

   b. Draw four quadrilaterals with unequal sides and connect the midpoints of adjacent sides. What kind of quadrilaterals appear to have been formed?

   ____

4. A penny with Lincoln's head upright is rolled along the edge of another penny as shown in the figure.

   a. At the end, do you think Lincoln will be right-side-up or upside-down?

   ____

   b. Conduct an experiment to find out. What are your results?

   ____

Practice

Surface Area—Prisms and Cylinders

Name the polyhedron and find the surface area of each net.

1. 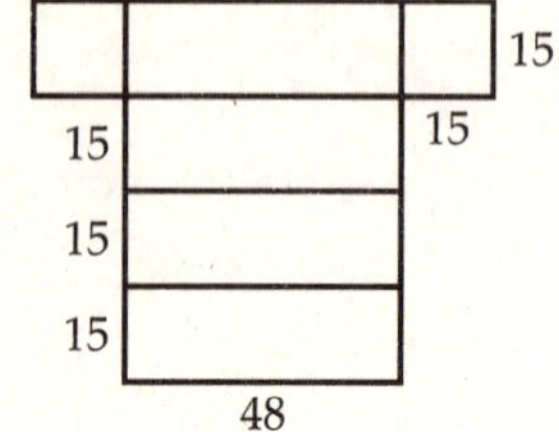

____

____

2. 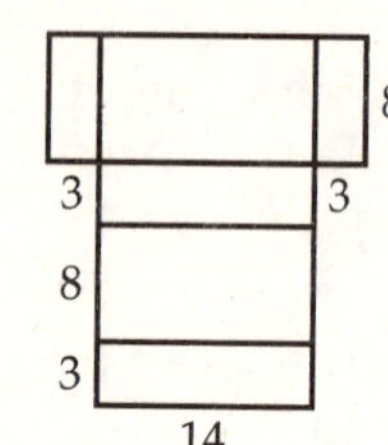

____

____

3. 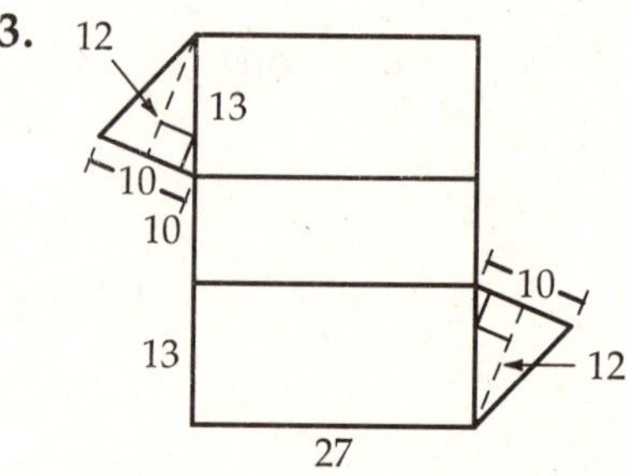

____

____

Draw and label a net and find the surface area. Use 3.14 for π.

4. 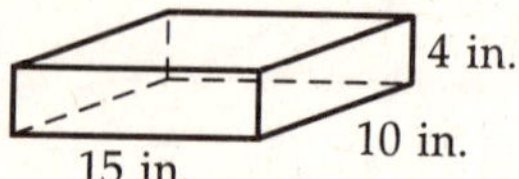

surface area = _______________________

5. 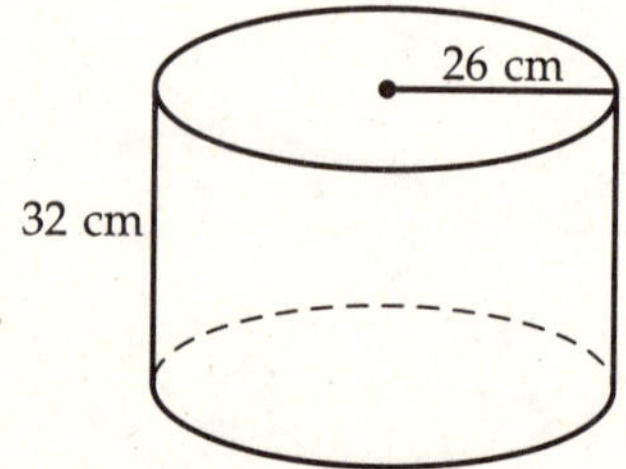

surface area = _______________________

Solve.

6. A room is 18 ft long, 14 ft wide, and 8 ft high.

   a. Find the cost of painting the four walls with two coats of paint costing \$9.50 per gallon. Each gallon covers 256 ft^2.

   ____

   b. Find the cost of carpeting the floor with carpet costing \$3/ft^2.

   ____

   c. Find the cost of covering the ceiling with acoustic tile costing \$7.50/ft^2.

   ____

   d. Find the total cost of renovating the room.

   ____

Chapter 10

Practice

Surface Area—Pyramids, Cones, and Spheres

Draw and label a net and find the surface area. Use 3.14 for π.

1. 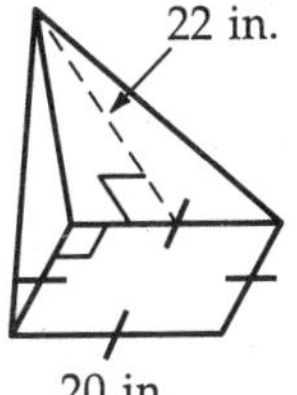

surface area = _________________

2. 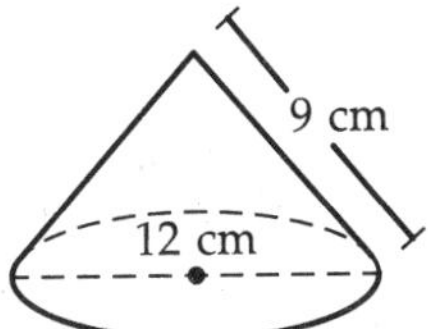

surface area = _________________

3. 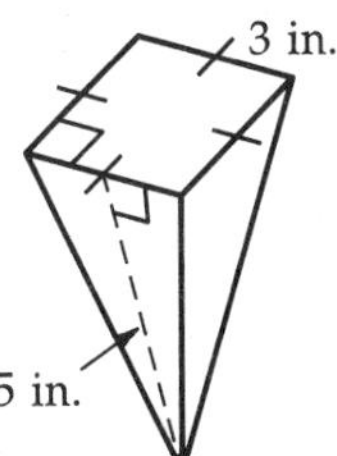

surface area = _________________

Find the surface area.
Give an exact answer.

4. A cone
   $d = 36$ in., $l = 50$ in.

   ____

5. A square-based pyramid
   $s = 8$ in., $l = 12$ in.

   ____

6. A cone
   $r = 64$ cm, $l = 90$ cm

   ____

7. A sphere with diameter 44 cm _________________

8. A hemisphere with radius 5 in. _________________

9. A sphere with radius 27 in. _________________

10. A hemisphere with diameter 70 cm _________________

11. A cone and a square-based pyramid have slant heights of
    6 in. The diameter for the cone and the base edge of the
    pyramid are both 8 in.

    a. Which space figure has the greater surface area? _________________

    b. By how much does the surface area of the greater space
       figure exceed that of the smaller? Use 3.14 for π.

    ____

Practice

Volume of Prisms and Cylinders

Find the volume of each prism.

1. rectangular base:
8 in. by 6 in.
height: 7 in.

____

2. square base:
3.5 ft on a side
height: 6 ft

____

3. cube:
sides: $13y$

____

4. 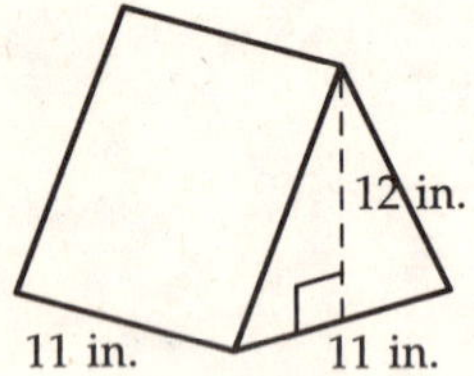

____

5. 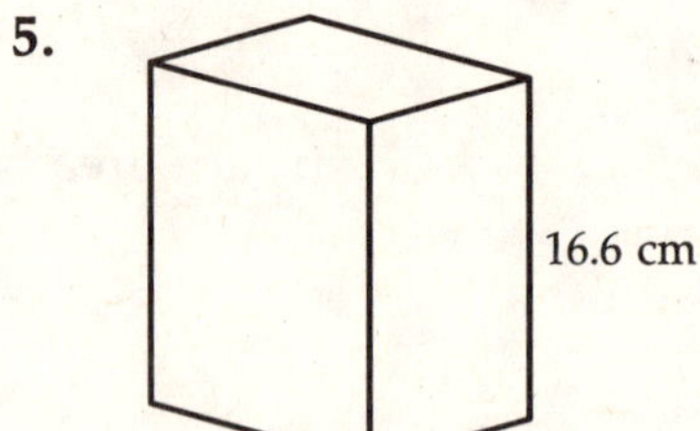

____

6. 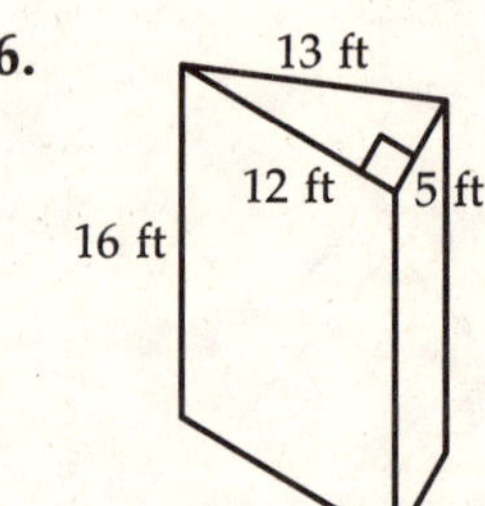

____

Find the volume of each cylinder.

7. radius: 14 in.
height: 18 in.

____

8. radius: 5.2 cm
height: 11.2 cm

____

9. diameter: 5 ft
height: 9 ft

____

10. 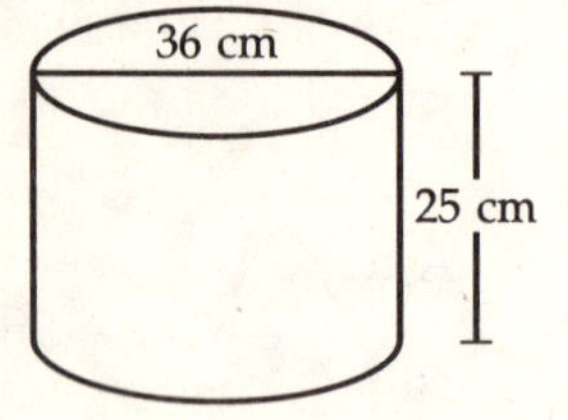

____

11. 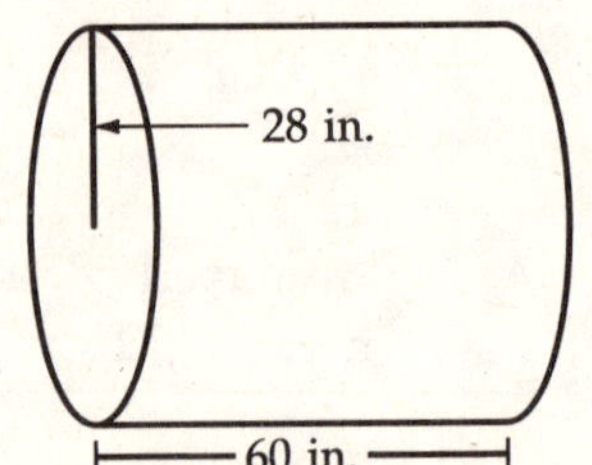

____

12. 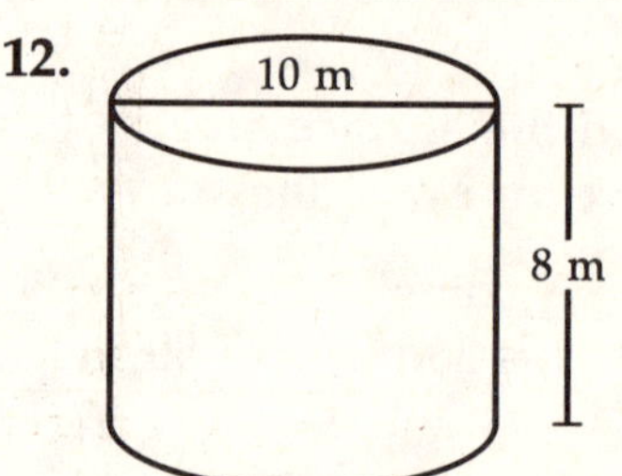

____

13. The height of a prism with volume 621 in.^{3} is 23 in. Find the area of the base.

____

14. Find the length of each side of a square-base prism if the height is 11 cm and the volume is 539 cm^3.

____

15. A cylinder has height 14 cm and volume $1{,}134\pi$ cm^3.

   a. Find the area of the base. _______________

   b. Find the radius. _______________

Practice

Volume of Pyramids, Cones, and Spheres

Find the volume. Use 3.14 for π.

1. square-based pyramid
$s = 9$ in.
$h = 12$ in.

____

2. cone
$r = 8$ cm
$h = 15$ cm

____

3. sphere
$r = 6$ in.

____

4. cone
$B = 93$ ft^2
$h = 7$ ft

____

5. sphere
$r = \frac{3}{4}$ in.

____

6. pyramid
$B = 774$ cm^2
$h = 42$ cm

____

7.
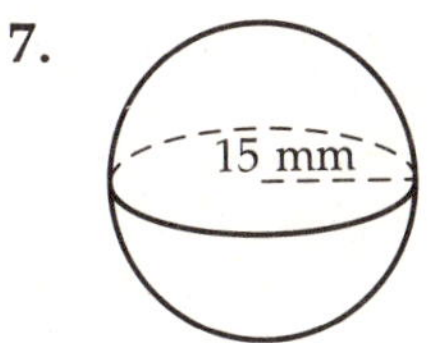

____

8.
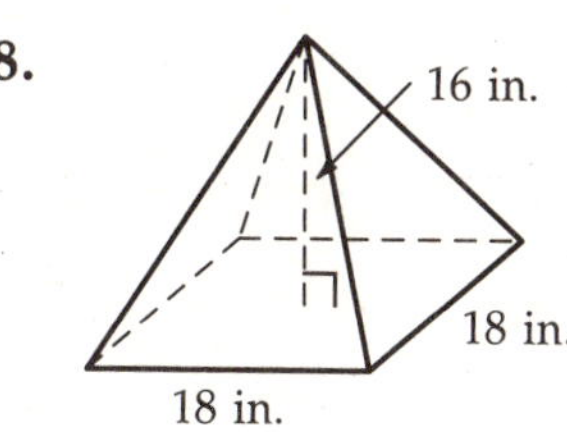

____

9.
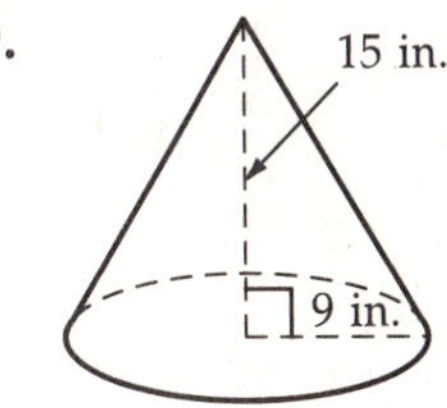

____

10. An ice-cream cone has radius 3 cm and height 12 cm. Ice cream fills the cone and forms a hemisphere at the opening. Find the total volume of ice cream. Use 3.14 for π.

____

11. A cone with base area 372 in.^{2} has volume 2,852 in.^{3}. Find the height of the cone.

____

12. Find the radius of a sphere that has volume $\frac{32}{3}\pi$ in.^{3}.

____

13. The base of a pyramid is a square with sides 12 in. long. The pyramid is 16 in. high. A cone has a radius of 6 in. and a height of 16 in.

a. Which figure has the greater volume?

____

b. The figure with greater volume is filled with sand and some of this sand is poured into the smaller figure. When the smaller figure is full, how much sand remains in the larger figure? Use 3.14 for π.

____

Practice

Finding Square Roots

True or false?

1. Negative numbers are neither rational nor irrational. _________

2. $p^2 = c$. Therefore, $c = \sqrt{p}$. _________

3. One square root of $\frac{16}{25}$ is $-\frac{4}{5}$. _________

4. $\sqrt{1}$ is an irrational number. _________

5. $\sqrt{29}$ is between 5 and 6. _________

6. A number that can be expressed as a repeating decimal is rational.

   ____

7. All real numbers are rational. _________

8. Every positive number has two square roots. _________

MENTAL MATH Square each term.

9. 15 _________   10. $\frac{1}{2}$ _________   11. 0.2 _________   12. -9 _________

13. y^3 _________   14. $\sqrt{7}$ _________   15. $3m$ _________   16. $\sqrt{a+b}$ _________

MENTAL MATH Simplify.

17. $\sqrt{900}$ _________   18. $\sqrt{x^{16}}$ _________   19. $\sqrt{144}$ _________   20. $\sqrt{9+16}$ _________

Find each square root. If necessary, use your calculator. Round decimal answers to the nearest thousandth.

21. $\sqrt{169}$ _________   22. $-\sqrt{100}$ _________   23. $\sqrt{0.16}$ _________

24. $\sqrt{1369}$ _________   25. $\sqrt{\frac{121}{144}}$ _________   26. $\sqrt{83.7}$ _________

27. $\sqrt{225x^8}$ _________   28. $\sqrt{(x+7)^{12}}$ _________   29. $\sqrt{18p^3 \cdot 2p}$ _________

30. $\sqrt{81x^{10}y^{14}}$ _________   31. $\sqrt{18 \cdot 8}$ _________   32. $\sqrt{343 \div 7}$ _________

Each square root is between what two integers? Circle the integer to which it is closer.

33. $\sqrt{18}$ _______ , _______   34. $\sqrt{60}$ _______ , _______   35. $-\sqrt{8}$ _______ , _______

36. $\sqrt{90}$ _______ , _______   37. $\sqrt{29+8}$ _______ , _______   38. $-\sqrt{21}$ _______ , _______

Is the term rational or irrational? Write R or I.

39. $\sqrt{289}$ _________   40. 5.7777… _________   41. $\sqrt{41}$ _________

Practice

Simulating a Problem

Solve by simulating the problem.

1. Twenty people seated in a circle counted to seven, beginning with the number one. The seventh person dropped out and those remaining counted to seven again. If every seventh person dropped out, what was the number of the last person remaining in the circle? Use the number circle to simulate the problem.

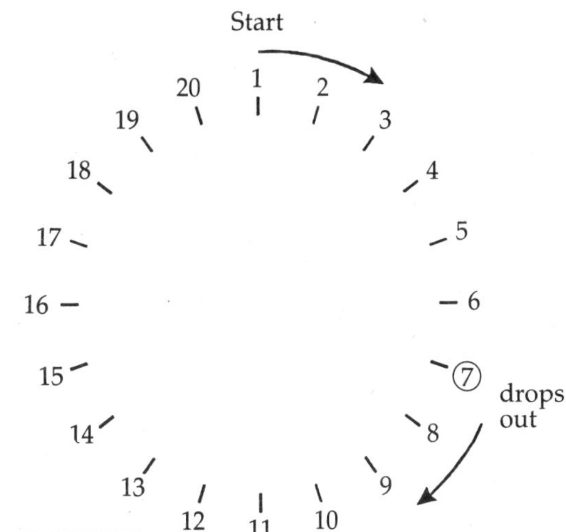

____

2. The two digits of Luther's age are the same. The tens' and ones' digits of his house number, which is between 400 and 500, show his age. His house number is divisible by his daughter's age, 13.

   a. Find the first number between 400 and 500 which is divisible by 13.

   ____

   b. By adding 13 successively, write the remaining numbers between 400 and 500 that are divisible by 13.

   ____

   c. Which of the numbers that you wrote is Luther's house number?

   ____

3. The Rockets played their first volleyball game on Friday, October 18, and played a game every Friday thereafter.

   a. What was the date of their ninth game? _______________________

   b. What was the number of the game they played on February 7?

   ____

4. Five coins are placed side by side as shown. A move consists of sliding two adjacent coins to an open spot without changing the order of the two coins. (The move "2-3 right" is illustrated.) Find three successive moves that will leave the coins in this order: 3-1-5-2-4

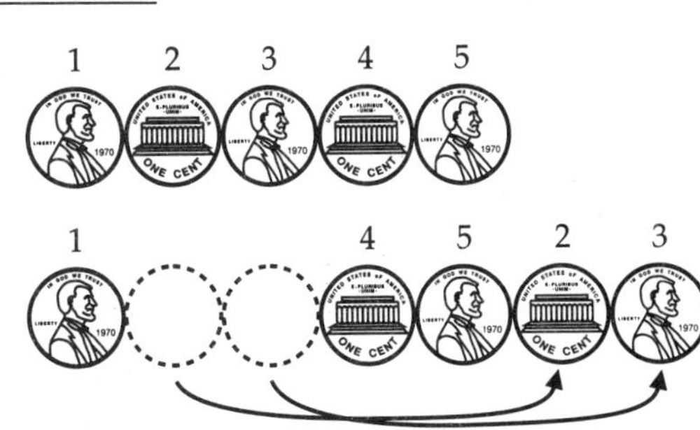

   ____

   ____

Practice

Pythagorean Theorem

CALCULATOR Find each value to the nearest thousandth.

1. $\sqrt{48}$ _________

2. $\sqrt{7}$ _________

3. $\sqrt{85}$ _________

Write an equation. Solve for x. Calculate each length to the nearest hundredth if the length is not a whole number.

4. 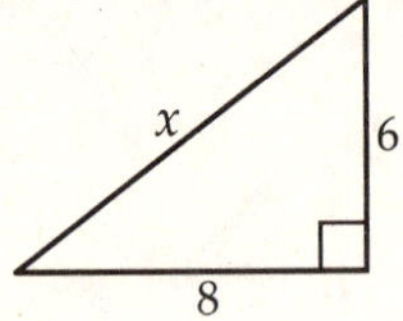

____

$x =$ _______________________

5. 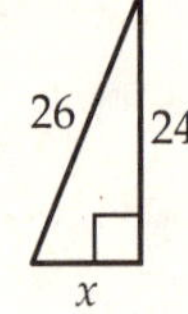

____

$x =$ _______________________

6. 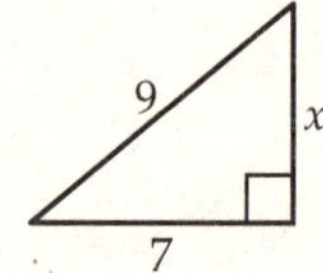

____

$x =$ _______________________

7. 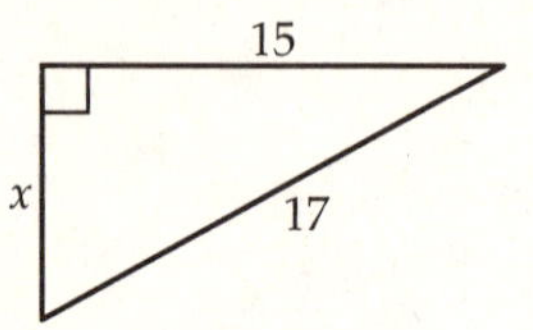

____

$x =$ _______________________

8. 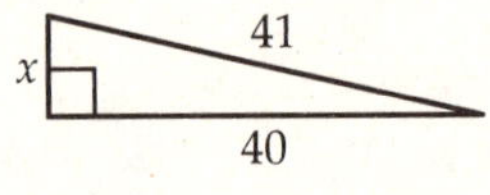

____

$x =$ _______________________

9. 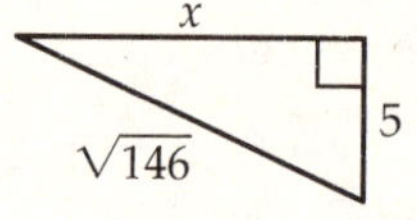

____

$x =$ _______________________

10. 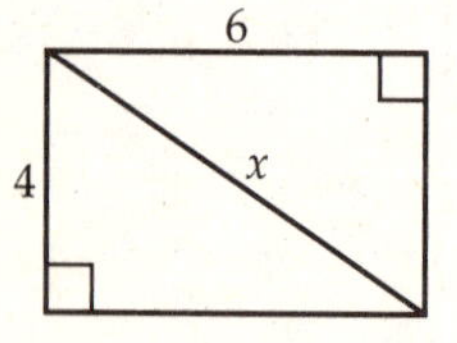

____

$x =$ _______________________

11. 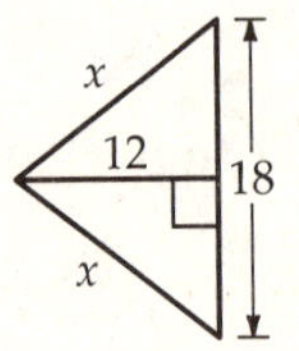

____

$x =$ _______________________

12. 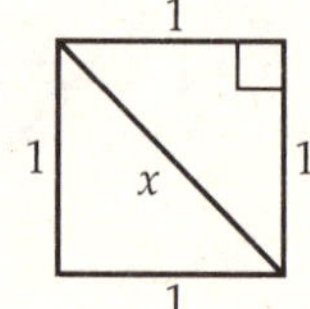

____

$x =$ _______________________

Determine which are Pythagorean triples. Write yes or no.

13. 20, 21, 29 _________

14. 7, 11, 12 _________

15. 10, $2\sqrt{11}$, 12 _________

16. 28, 45, 53 _________

17. $m, n, \sqrt{m^2 + n^2}$ _________

18. 10, 15, 20 _________

19. A rectangular park measures 300 ft by 400 ft. A sidewalk runs diagonally from one corner to the opposite corner. Find the length of the sidewalk.

____

Practice

Similar Right Triangles

MENTAL MATH Solve for variable x.

1. $\dfrac{3}{4} = \dfrac{15}{x}$

$x =$ _________

2. $\dfrac{x}{6} = \dfrac{6}{9}$

$x =$ _________

3. $\dfrac{9}{24} = \dfrac{6}{x}$

$x =$ _________

4. $\dfrac{3}{x} = \dfrac{12}{20}$

$x =$ _________

Solve for variable x using the Pythagorean theorem. Use the square root table to find the length to the nearest thousandth.

5. 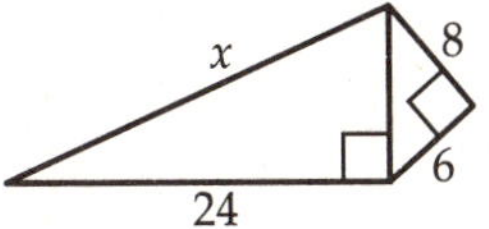

____

6. 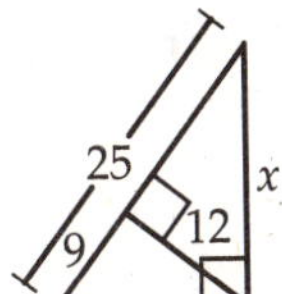

____

7. 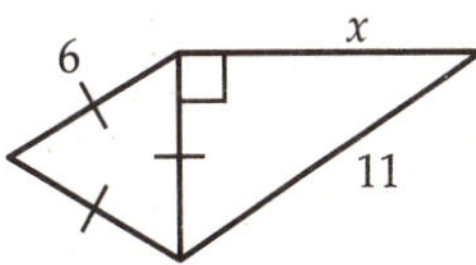

____

Solve for variable x. Each pair of triangles is similar.

8. 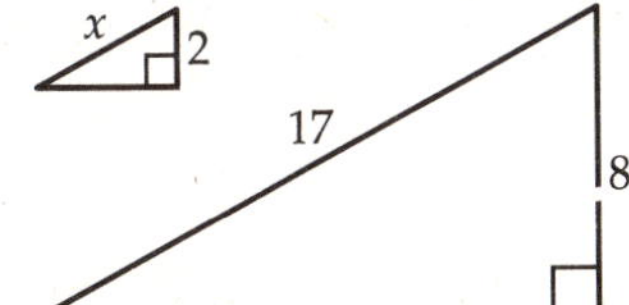

____

9. 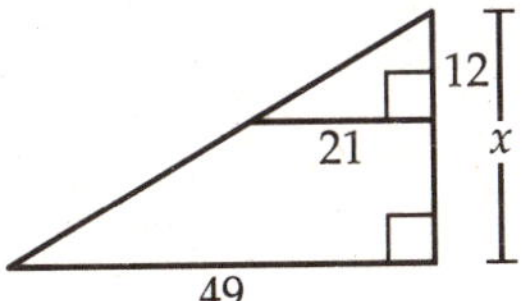

____

10. 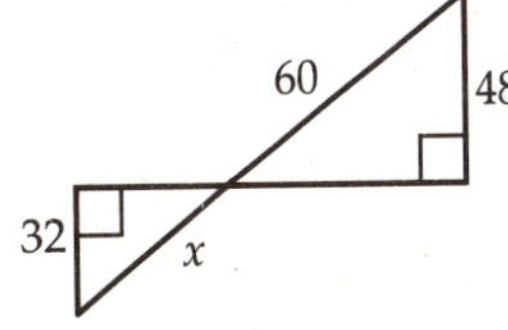

____

CALCULATOR Solve for x and y. Round each decimal answer to the nearest hundredth.

11. 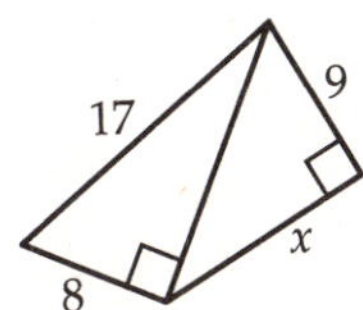

$x =$ _________

12. 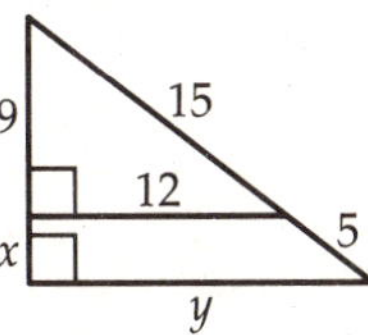

$x =$ _________

$y =$ _________

13. 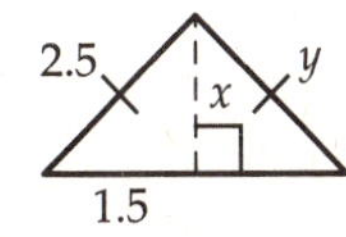

$x =$ _________

$y =$ _________

Find the measures of the indicated angles.

14. $\angle B$ _________

15. $\angle 1$ _________

16. $\angle 2$ _________

17. Why is $\triangle ACD \sim \triangle CBD$? _______________________________________

18. Why is $\triangle CBD \sim \triangle ABC$? _______________________________________

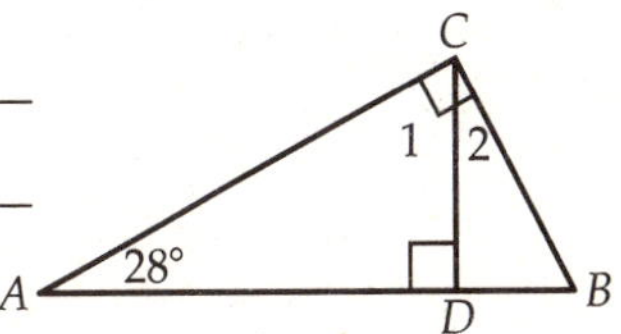

Practice

Special Right Triangles

Use the triangle to answer each question.

1. Which side is opposite $\angle W$? _________

2. Which side is opposite $\angle G$? _________

3. Which side is opposite $\angle M$? _________

4. Which sides are legs? _____________

5. Which side is the hypotenuse? _________

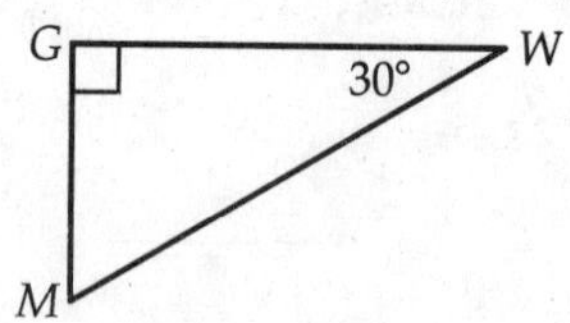

The length of one side of the triangle is given. Find the missing measures. Answers may contain square root signs.

	m	n	p
6.	14		
7.			36
8.		$9\sqrt{3}$	
9.	5		

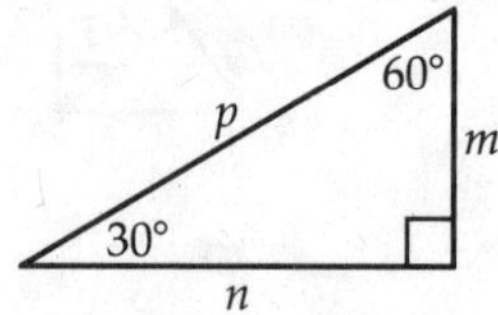

	x	y	z
10.	11		
11.		8.7	
12.			$7\sqrt{2}$
13.	17		

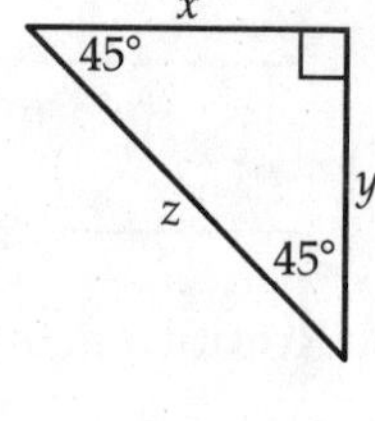

In the figure, $BD = 6\sqrt{2}$. Find each value.

14. AB _________

15. AD _________

16. BC _________

17. CD _________

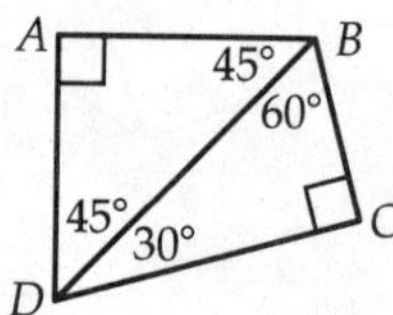

18. **MENTAL MATH** One leg of a 45°-45°-90° right triangle measures 14 cm. Find the perimeter.

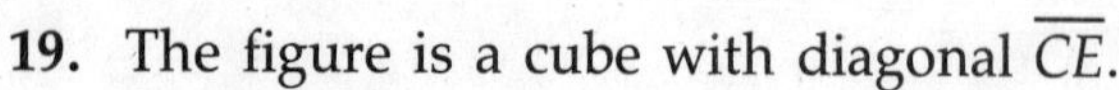

____

19. The figure is a cube with diagonal $\overline{CE}$.

   a. Find CG. _____________

   b. Find GE. _____________

   c. Use the Pythagorean theorem in $\triangle CGE$ to find CE to the nearest tenth.

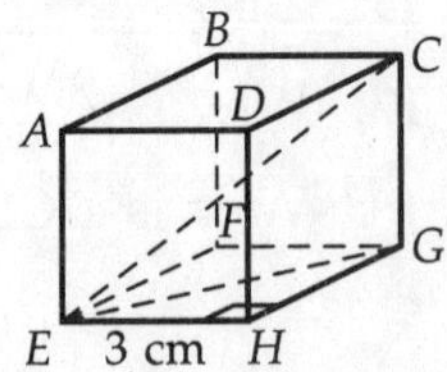

■ Practice

For use after 11-6 (pp. 473–476)

Trigonometric Ratios

Use the table of trigonometric ratios to find each value.

1. cos 20° _________
2. tan 64° _________
3. sin 41° _________

4. tan 8° _________
5. sin 88° _________
6. cos 53° _________

Find $m\angle A$.

7. tan A = 5.1446 _________
8. sin A = 0.0872 _________
9. cos A = 0.3746 _________

MENTAL MATH **Write each ratio using square root signs. Use your knowledge of 45°-45°-90° and 30°-60°-90° right triangles.**

10. tan 30° _________
11. cos 45° _________
12. sin 60° _________

Find the trigonometric ratios.

13. sin N _________
14. tan M _________

15. cos N _________

Write the trigonometric ratio to the nearest hundredth.

16. sin B _________
17. cos B _________

18. tan A _________

Find x, y, and z for each triangle. Write each decimal answer to the nearest hundredth.

19. x = _________

y = _________

z = _________

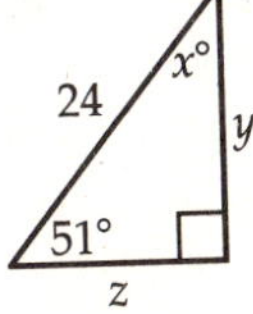

20. x = _________

y = _________

z = _________

21. x = _________

y = _________

z = _________

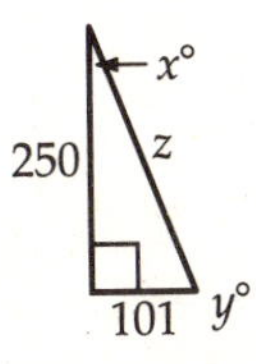

22. x = _________

y = _________

z = _________

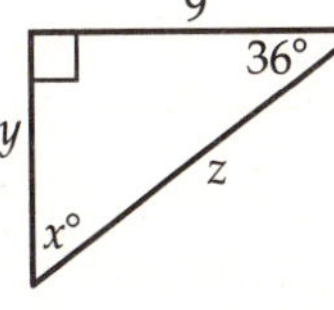

23. A surveyor standing 2,250 ft from the base of the World Trade Center in New York City measured a 31° angle to the topmost point. To the nearest ft, how tall is the World Trade Center?

____

Practice

For use after 12-1 (pp. 488–491)

Mean, Median, and Mode

Complete for the given sets of data.

Data	Mean	Median	Mode	Range
1. 8, 15, 9, 7, 4, 5, 9, 11	_______	_______	_______	_______
2. 70, 61, 28, 40, 60, 72, 25, 31, 64, 63	_______	_______	_______	_______
3. 4.9, 5.7, 6.0, 5.3, 4.8, 4.9, 5.3, 4.7, 4.9, 5.6, 5.1	_______	_______	_______	_______
4. 271, 221, 234, 240, 271, 234, 213, 253, 196	_______	_______	_______	_______
5. 0, 2, 3, 3, 3, 4, 4, 5	_______	_______	_______	_______
6. $\frac{5}{8}, \frac{1}{2}, \frac{1}{4}, \frac{1}{8}$	_______	_______	_______	_______
7. 1,216; 4,891; 2,098; 3,662; 5,748	_______	_______	_______	_______
8. 1, 2, 3, 4, 5, 6, 7, 8, 9, 10	_______	_______	_______	_______
9. 5, 10, 15, 20, 25, 30, 35, 40	_______	_______	_______	_______
10. 85, 73, 93, 74, 71, 101, 71, 90, 98	_______	_______	_______	_______

11. There were 8 judges at a gymnastics competition. Kathleen received these scores for her performance on the uneven parallel bars:

$$8.9, 8.7, 8.9, 9.2, 8.8, 8.2, 8.9, 8.8$$

a. Find these statistics: mean _________ median _________ mode _________

b. Which statistic reflects a typical score? Explain.

____

____

c. Why do you think that the highest and lowest judge's scores are disregarded in tallying the total score in a gymnastics competition?

____

____

Chapter 12

Practice

Line Plots and Frequency Tables

Draw a line plot for each frequency distribution. Find the
mean, the median, and the mode.

1.

x	1	2	3	4	5	6
f	2	0	4	1	2	4

mean ________

median ________

mode ________

```
1   2   3   4   5   6
```

2.

x	1	2	3	4	5	6
f	4	4	0	0	3	2

mean ________

median ________

mode ________

```
1   2   3   4   5   6
```

Make a frequency table for each set of data. Find the mean, the
median, and the mode.

3.   5 1 4 6 2 6 4 5
         1 3 2 6 4 5 4 6

mean ________

median ________

mode ________

4.   4 3 1 2 1 3
         3 6 1 3 2 1

mean ________

median ________

mode ________

Construct the frequency table from each of the following line
plots. Find the mean, the median, and the mode.

5.

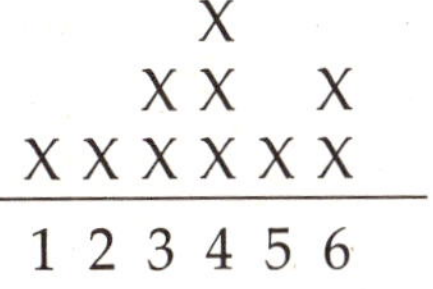

mean ________

median ________

mode ________

▰ *Practice*

For use after 12-3 (pp. 498–501)

Stem and Leaf Plots

Make a stem and leaf plot for each set of data, then find the median and the mode.

1. 50, 39, 40, 48, 38, 42, 53, 42,
   38, 48, 47, 43, 51, 48, 43

   median _________ mode _________

2. 6.2, 7.0, 6.3, 6.6, 7.2, 7.3, 6.7, 7.2, 7.0,
   6.1, 6.7, 6.4, 6.9, 7.2, 6.2, 6.8, 7.1

   median _________ mode _________

3. 14, 19, 23, 30, 26, 10, 7, 16, 28, 17,
   24, 1, 28, 19, 10, 16, 19, 5, 25

   median _________ mode _________

4. 91, 106, 86, 93, 100, 84, 108, 95, 99,
   98, 83, 96, 109, 84, 105, 102, 87, 94

   median _________ mode _________

Make a back-to-back stem and leaf plot from each of the sets of data. Then find the median and the mode for each set of data.

5. Set A: 25, 28, 31, 20, 26,
           22, 21, 25

   Set B: 31, 28, 19, 20, 22,
           30, 18, 25, 27, 19

   A: median _________ mode _________

   B: median _________ mode _________

6. Set A: 175, 186, 169, 180,
           178, 183, 176, 184, 179

   Set B: 191, 175, 178, 187,
           180, 178, 186, 182, 179

   A: median _________ mode _________

   B: median _________ mode _________

Practice

Box and Whisker Plots

**Make a box and whisker plot for each set
of data.**

1. 16, 20, 30, 15, 23, 11, 15,
    21, 30, 29, 13, 16

2. 9, 12, 10, 3, 2, 3, 9, 11, 5,
    1, 10, 4, 7, 12, 3, 10

3. 70, 77, 67, 65, 79, 82, 70, 68,
    75, 73, 69, 66, 70, 73, 89, 72

Use the box and whisker plot to answer each question.

Weekly Mileage Totals, 24 Runners

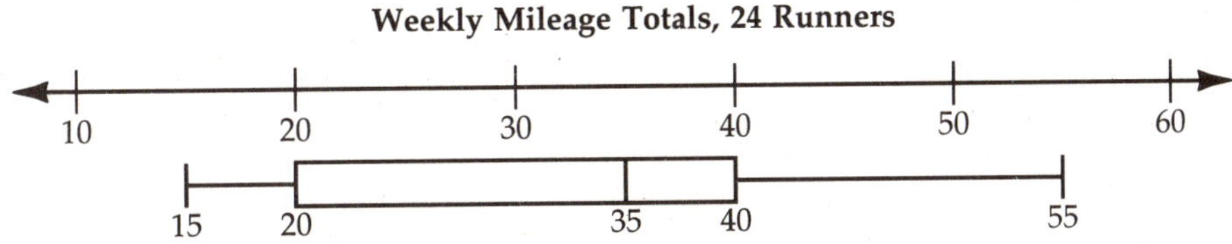

4. What is the highest weekly total? _________ the lowest? _________

5. What is the median weekly total? _________

6. What percent of runners run less than 40 miles a week? _________

7. How many runners run less than 20 miles a week? _________

WRITE **Make a box and whisker plot for each set of data. Use a
single number line. Then write a comparison.**

8. 1st set: 7, 12, 25, 3, 1, 29, 30, 7, 15, 2,
             5, 10, 29, 1, 10, 30, 18, 8, 7, 29

    2nd set: 37, 17, 14, 43, 27, 19, 32, 1, 8, 48,
             26, 16, 28, 6, 25, 18

____

____

____

____

Practice

Counting Principle

Find the value of each factorial.

1. $3!$ _________

2. $6!$ _________

3. $4!$ _________

4. $\frac{7!}{5!}$ _________

5. $\frac{8!}{7!}$ _________

6. $\frac{6!}{2!}$ _________

7. $\frac{3!}{4!}$ _________

8. $\frac{12!}{10!}$ _________

CALCULATOR Find the value of each factorial.

9. $11!$ ________________

10. $4! \times 7!$ ________________

11. $\frac{13!}{5!}$ ________________

12. $\frac{5!8!}{6!}$ ________________

MENTAL MATH Find the value of each factorial.

13. $\frac{5!}{3!}$ _________

14. $\frac{18!}{17!}$ _________

15. $\frac{11!}{9!}$ _________

16. $\frac{8!}{6!}$ _________

Solve each problem using a tree diagram.

17. A ballot offered 3 choices, for president (A, B, C) and 2 choices for vice president (M, N). How many choices for a combination of the two offices did it offer? List them.

____

18. The Cougar baseball team has 4 pitchers ($P1$, $P2$, $P3$, $P4$) and 2 catchers ($C1$, $C2$). How many pitcher-catcher combinations are possible? List them.

____

Solve each problem using the counting principle.

19. There are 5 roads from Allen to Baker, 7 roads from Baker to Carlson, and 4 roads from Carlson to Dodge. How many different routes from Allen to Dodge by way of Baker and Carlson are possible?

____

20. Drapery is sold in 4 different fabrics. Each fabric comes in 13 different patterns. Each pattern is offered in 9 different colors. How many fabric-pattern-color combinations are there?

____

Practice

Probability

Find each probability.

1. A letter is chosen at random from the word PROBABILITY.
   Find the probability of each event.

   a. selecting a *B* _________

   b. selecting a *P* _________

   c. selecting an *A* or an *I* _________

   d. not selecting a *P* _________

2. A child is chosen at random from the Erb and Smith
   families. Find the probability that the child is:

	Erb family	Smith family
Girls	2	5
Boys	4	3

   a. a boy _________

   b. an Erb _________

   c. an Erb girl _________

   d. a child _________

   e. not a Jones boy _________

   f. a Jones _________

3. A spinner numbered from 1 to 20 is spun randomly. Find
   the probability that the spinner lands on:

   a. 17 _________

   b. an odd number _________

   c. a number divisible by 5 _________

   d. 26 _________

   e. a number with a 1 in it _________

   f. a prime number _________

   g. a square number _________

   h. a number _________

   i. a number that is not less than 17 _________

   j. a number divisible by 3 or 4 _________

4. A drawer contains 6 red socks, 4 blue socks, and 14 white socks.
   A sock is pulled from the drawer at random. Find the
   probability that the sock is:

   a. red _________

   b. blue _________

   c. red or white _________

   d. red, white, or blue _________

   e. not red _________

   f. green _________

5. A box contains 7 red, 14 yellow, 21 green, 42 blue, and 84
   purple marbles. A marble is drawn at random from the box.
   Find the probability that the marble is:

   a. red _________

   b. yellow _________

   c. green or blue _________

   d. purple, yellow, or red _________

Practice

For use after 12-7 (pp. 518–520)

Simulate the Problem

1. Suppose that before the 1999 World Series you attempt to predict the winners of the seven games. What is the probability that you will get 4 or more out of 7 correct?

   Model the situation using a coin. Let heads represent Red Sox and tails represent Cubs. A trial occurs when you toss the coin seven times to represent the seven games in the series. A successful trial occurs when you get four or more outcomes that match the true outcomes listed in the table.

   Work with a partner. Carry out 50 trials. Write the probability after the given number of trials.

1999 World Series	
Game	**Winner**
1	Red Sox
2	Cubs
3	Red Sox
4	Cubs
5	Cubs
6	Red Sox
7	Red Sox

   a. 10 __________

   b. 20 __________

   c. 30 __________

   d. 40 __________

   e. 50 __________

2. An irresponsible TV weatherperson forecasts the weather by throwing a number cube and consulting the weather key shown here. The weather during one 5-day stretch is given in the table. What is the probability that the forecaster was right at least 3 days out of 5?

   Weather Key

   1—clear and warm
   2—clear and cool
   3—cloudy and cool
   4—intermittent showers
   5—continual rain
   6—snow

   Use a number cube to simulate the forecaster's predictions. A successful trial occurs when you roll the correct weather three or more times out of five.

Mon	Tue	Wed	Thu	Fri
continual rain	continual rain	clear and cool	cloudy and cool	snow

   Work with a partner. Carry out 50 trials. Write the probability after the given number of trials.

   a. 10 __________

   b. 20 __________

   c. 30 __________

   d. 40 __________

   e. 50 __________

Chapter 12

Practice

Independent and Dependent Events

Determine whether each of the pairs of events is independent or dependent. Write *I* or *D* and explain.

1. A guest at a party takes a sandwich from a tray. A second guest then takes a sandwich.

   ____

2. Sam flips a coin and gets heads. He flips again and gets tails.

   ____

For each exercise, assume that events *A and B* are independent. Then find *P(A and B)*.

3. $P(A) = \frac{2}{3}$, and $P(B) = \frac{3}{4}$ _________

4. $P(A) = \frac{1}{2}$, and $P(B) = \frac{8}{9}$ _________

5. $P(A) = \frac{5}{14}$, and $P(B) = \frac{7}{15}$ _________

6. $P(A) = 1$, and $P(B) = 0$ _________

Determine whether each problem involves dependent or independent events. Then find the probability.

7. A shelf holds 3 novels, 2 biographies and 1 history book. Two students in turn choose a book at random. What is the probability that the students chose each of the following? ________________

   a. both novels _________

   b. both biographies _________

   c. a history, then a novel _________

   d. a novel, then a history _________

8. Meg flipped a penny the given number of times. What is the probability the results were as follows?

   ____

   a. 2; two heads _________

   b. 2; two tails _________

   c. 2; a tail, then a head _________

   d. 5; five tails _________

9. Two puppies are chosen at random from a box at the mall. What is the probability of these outcomes?

   ____

Free Puppies for Adoption!
5 black retrievers
3 brown hounds
4 black setters

   a. both black _________

   b. both brown _________

   c. a setter, then a hound _________

   d. a retriever, then a setter _________

   e. both setters _________

■■■ *Practice*

Polynomials

Tell whether the expression is a monomial. Write *yes* or *no*.

1. n _______

2. $7 - 3m - m^2$ _______

3. $\frac{1}{x}$ _______

4. $7.27k^9$ _______

5. $1,000$ _______

6. $\frac{1}{9}x^2y^4z$ _______

Identify each expression as a monomial, binomial, or trinomial. Write *m*, *b*, or *t*.

7. $36abc$ _______

8. $10 - h^3$ _______

9. $95xy + y$ _______

10. $a^2 + b^2 + cd$ _______

11. $3k$ _______

12. $-12e + 12f^2$ _______

Model each polynomial.

13. $x^2 + 2x + 2$

14. $2x^2 + x + 1$

Write the polynomial for each model.

15. 

____

16. 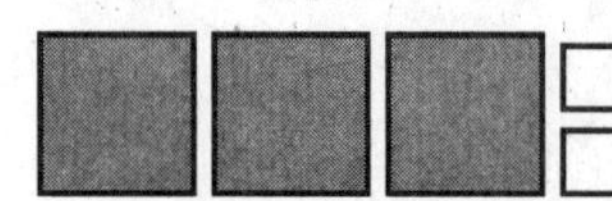

____

17. 

____

18. 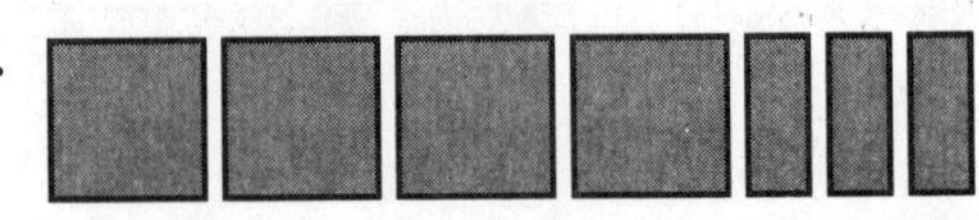

____

MENTAL MATH Evaluate each polynomial for $x = {}^-1$, $y = 3$, and $z = 2$.

19. $x^2 + z$ _______

20. $3y + x$ _______

21. $2z + y$ _______

22. $x + y + z$ _______

23. $x^2 + y^2$ _______

24. $z - x - y$ _______

CALCULATOR Evaluate each polynomial for $m = 21$, $n = {}^-9$, and $p = 28$.

25. $3m - 2p$ _______

26. $2n^2 - 5m$ _______

27. $m^2 - n^2$ _______

28. $n^2 + 5n - 6$ _______

29. $5p^2 - 5p$ _______

30. $7m + 6p$ _______

Practice

Adding and Subtracting Polynomials

Use a model to find each sum.

1. $(2x^2 + 5x + 4) + (x^2 - 3x - 3)$ _________________________

2. $(-x^2 + 3x - 1) + (3x^2 - x + 2)$ _________________________

Find each sum by combining like terms.

3. $(5x + 3) + (2x - 7)$ _________________________

4. $2x^2 + 4 + (3x^2 - 4x - 5)$ _________________________

5. $(-2x^2 + 4x - 5) + (8x + 5x^2 + 6)$ _________________________

6. $4x^2 + 1 + (3x - 5x^2 - 2)$ _________________________

7. $\begin{aligned} 6x^2 + \ 5x - \ 5 \\ + \ x^2 - \ \ 8x + \ 3 \end{aligned}$ _________________________

8. $\begin{aligned} 2x^3 - \ 5x^2 \qquad\qquad -5 \\ +3x^3 + \ 7x^2 \ + \ 9x \end{aligned}$ _________________________

9. $\begin{aligned} -4x^2y^2 + \ 3xy \ + x^2 - \ 4y^2 \\ + \ \ x^2y^2 - \ 6xy \ - x^2 - \ 5y^2 \end{aligned}$ _________________________

10. $\begin{aligned} 12x^2y + \ 9xy^2 - \ 2x^2 + \ 5y^2 \\ + \ \ x^2y - \ 8xy^2 + \ 2x^2 - \ \ y^2 \end{aligned}$ _________________________

Use a model to find each difference.

11. $(3x - 2) - (4x + 3)$ _________________________

12. $(2x^2 - 4x + 1) - (x^2 - 2x + 1)$ _________________________

Subtract each pair of polynomials by adding the opposite of the second polynomial.

13. $(10m - 4) - (3m - 5)$ _________________________

14. $(k^2 - 2k + 5) - (k^2 + 5k + 3)$ _________________________

15. $(2x^2 + 7x - 4) - (x^2 - 4)$ _________________________

16. $(3x^2y^2 + 2xy + 5y) - (-2x^2y^2 - 4x + 5y)$ _________________________

17. $(7x^3 - 5x^2 - 3x + 8) - (10x^3 - 4x^2 + 5x + 9)$ _________________________

18. $(x^2 + 2y + 5) - (4x + 4y)$ _________________________

19. $(-4a^2b + 7ab^2 - 9a - 6b + 13) - (-6a^2b + 8a + 10b - 18)$

____

Practice

Multiplying a Polynomial by a Monomial

Use a model to find each product.

1. $x(4x + 2)$ _____________
2. $x(3x - 2)$ _____________
3. $2x(x - 2)$ _____________
4. $3x(x + 5)$ _____________
5. $2x(3x + 1)$ _____________
6. $3x(3x - 1)$ _____________

CALCULATOR Find each product. Then evaluate the expression for $x = -9$ and $y = 14$.

7. $x^2(x + 2y)$ _____________
8. $-xy(2x - y)$ _____________
9. $y(4x + y - 2x^2)$ _____________
10. $3y(5y - 2x + 4xy)$ _____________

Use the distributive property to simplify.

11. $4x(3x - 5)$ _____________
12. $-8x(x - 7)$ _____________
13. $6y(x^2 + 2y)$ _____________
14. $7xy^2(y - 2x + x^2)$ _____________
15. $3xy(2xy + 5)$ _____________
16. $-9xyz(-2xy + 3yz - 4xz)$ _____________
17. $-\frac{1}{2}m(4m^2 - 2mn)$ _____________
18. $12ab(-\frac{1}{2}b + \frac{1}{4}a^3)$ _____________
19. $-15a^2(a - b + 3c)$ _____________
20. $-3x^2a^2(2a^3 + ab - x)$ _____________
21. $3x(2x - 4y) + 4y(3x - y)$ _____________
22. $x(5x + 2y + 4xy) - 3y(2x - 4x^2 + 3y)$ _____________

Write an expression for the area of each figure. Simplify.

23. 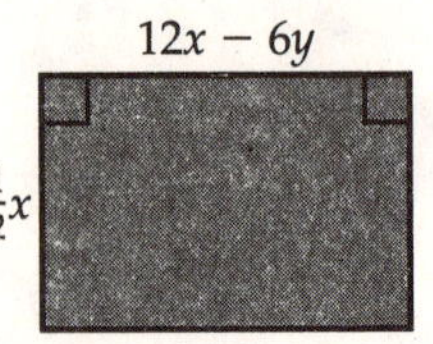

24. 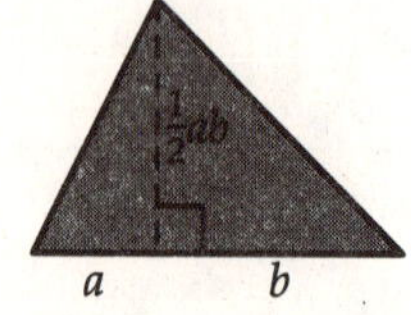

25. 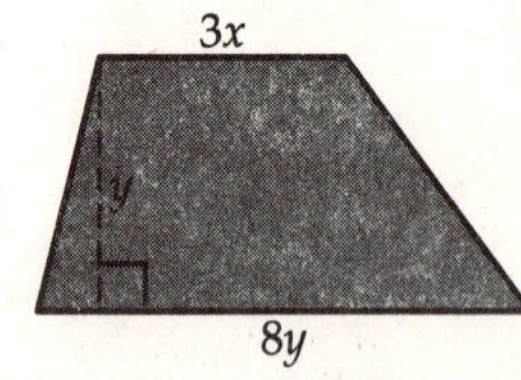

_____________ _____________ _____________

Practice

Multiplying Binomials

Find each product using models.

1. $(x + 2)(x + 3)$ _______________________

2. $(x + 5)(x + 1)$ _______________________

Find each product using the distributive property.

3. $(x + 4)(x + 5)$ _______________________

4. $(x + 7)(x + 2)$ _______________________

5. $(x + 1)(x - 6)$ _______________________

6. $(x + 8)(x - 3)$ _______________________

7. $(2x + 5)(x + 3)$ _______________________

8. $(x - 4)(x - 6)$ _______________________

Find each product using FOIL.

9. $(y - 7)(y - 6)$ _______________________

10. $(x - 9)(x - 5)$ _______________________

11. $(x - 10)(x + 3)$ _______________________

12. $(2x + 3)(3x + 2)$ _______________________

13. $(4x - 1)(2x + 7)$ _______________________

14. $(x + a)(x + b)$ _______________________

Find each product

15. $(y - 9)^2$ _______________________

16. $(x - 4)(x + 4)$ _______________________

17. $(3m - n)(m + n)$ _______________________

18. $(a - 14)(a + 8)$ _______________________

19. $(k - 6)(k + 6)$ _______________________

20. $(p + 5)^2$ _______________________

21. $(2x - 7)(2x + 7)$ _______________________

22. $(m - 15)(m - 20)$ _______________________

23. $(3k + 4)^2$ _______________________

24. $(x - 20)(x + 20)$ _______________________

25. $(5n + 4)(4n - 5)$ _______________________

26. $(10x - 1)^2$ _______________________

MENTAL MATH Find each product mentally.

27. $(x + 2)(x - 2)$ _______________________

28. $(x - 3)^2$ _______________________

29. $(a + b)(a - b)$ _______________________

30. $(x + 1)^2$ _______________________

31. $(a - b)(a - b)$ _______________________

32. $(x + 4)(x - 4)$ _______________________

33. A rectangle has length $4x + 3$ and height $3x - 7$. Find the area of the rectangle.

____

34. Mark worked for $6d - 9$ days and earned $8d + 25$ dollars per day. How much did he earn altogether?

____

Practice

Using Multiple Strategies

Solve.

1. The product of two whole numbers is 36. What is the greatest possible sum that the numbers can have?

____

2. The sum of two numbers is 14. What is the greatest possible product that the numbers can have?

____

3. A rectangle has length $(x - 3)^2$ and width 4. The perimeter of the rectangle is 40. Find the length.

____

4. A rectangle has length $k + 6$ and width $k - 6$. The area of the rectangle is 64. Find the length and the width.

____

5. A rectangular prism has length $x + 2$, width $x + 1$, height 4, and volume 24. Find the length and the width.

____

6. A piece of cardboard measures 12 ft by 12 ft. Corners are to be cut from it as shown by the broken lines, and the sides folded up to make a box with an open top. What size corners should be cut from the cardboard to make a box with the greatest possible volume?

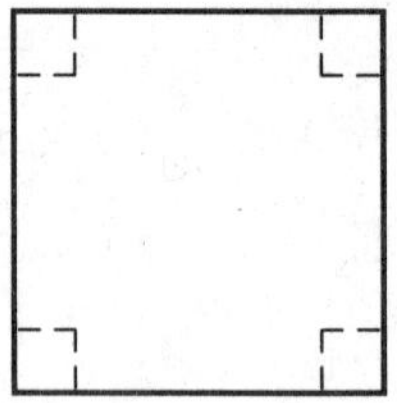

____

7. What is the maximum number of small boxes that can fit inside the large box?

____

8. The perimeter of a right triangle is 24 in. Find the dimensions of the triangle if the sides are all whole-number lengths.

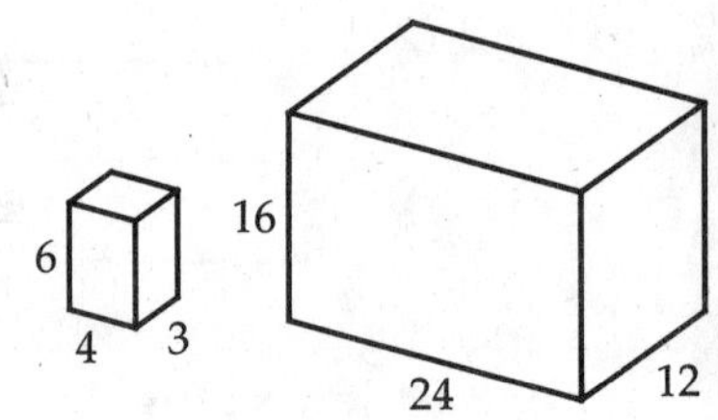

____